HOLY

Places, Small Spaces

A Hopeful Future for the Small Membership Church

Bill Kemp

DISCIPLESHIP
RESOURCES
PO BOX 340003
NASHVILLE TN
37203-0003
www.discipleshipresources.org

With gratitude to the laity of Bairdford United Methodist Church for their inspiration in writing this book.

Cover and book design by Nanci H. Lamar

ISBN 0-88177-456-1

Library of Congress Control Number 2004112416

DR456

Table of Contents

INTRODUCTION

A Hopeful Future

At the 2004 General Conference of the United Methodist Church, a caucus group began passing out stickers to the delegates with the question, "What is 52?" There were puzzled looks until the caucus revealed that half of the denomination's congregations had 52 or fewer people in weekly worship attendance. Any other Protestant denomination could have witnessed a similar demonstration at judicatory meetings. Whether one speaks about Baptists, Presbyterians, Episcopalians, or Lutherans, none have a median church attendance exceeding 125.[1]

This statistical benchmark is easily forgotten when you attend the national gatherings for these denominations. In the above mentioned General Conference of United Methodist Church, four out of every five delegates were from churches with more than two hundred members, and half of these delegates were from megachurches with more than 1,000 members.[2] These delegates were entrusted with decisions affecting the broad range of congregations, and yet many had never experienced worship in the average-sized church of the denomination. They were oblivious to how some legislation, like a slotted spoon passing through vegetable soup, misses the needs of the smaller church while capturing the hopes of those of a more noticeable size.

Very few of these predominately metro and suburban representatives can articulate or appreciate the differences between their own values and those held by the rural folk and the inner city poor that are served by small membership churches. For the small churches of our land to have a hopeful future, I believe that there needs to be an intentional inclusion of their representatives and a re-tuning of our ears to hear this still small voice.

This book seeks not only to affirm the importance of small membership churches, but also to discern the problems and the myths which if addressed will return the small membership church to its rightful place at the center of Christian outreach to our contemporary culture. My hope is to not only survey the landscape, but provide several simple concepts, which will aid small church leaders make their churches vital and sustainable.

Doing this will require answering the following questions:

How do we find a middle way between stagnation and growth, so that a congregation of 35, 50, or 100, can continue to have a vital ministry without needing to transition to a larger, less intimate, fellowship?

What is distinctive about the small church and is it reasonable to call a gathering of fifteen or twenty souls a "church?"

What toolbox of skills do small church leaders, both laity and pastors, need in order to remain effective in the new millennium?

How can the small membership church be provided with effective and affordable pastoral leadership? Is there a better way to train and support those who find themselves leading small churches?

What hopeful future is there for the small membership church in today's world of business mergers and school district consolidation?

How can small membership church rediscover a sense of their own mission, so that they are passionate about being what Christ calls them to be?

If these questions interest you, then read on. As a person who loves the small church, I cannot explore these issues without a sounding a note of criticism, as well as a sobering reality check. My criticism is directed towards the culture of nearly all of the mainline denominational organizations, which, regardless of their polity or theology, have focused for the last sixty years on lifting the professional standards of their clergy rather than on enhancing the spiritual passion and leadership capabilities of their laity. The sobering reality check centers on the hyper-inflationary costs of paying for a pastor and maintaining a small church during the current era of falling church attendance.

I believe the small membership church has a hopeful future. In many smaller congregations I have found a spiritual vitality and personal involvement of the membership that is both winsome and biblical. Those small membership churches that survive into next decade will find themselves in strategic places. They will occupy the physical and spiritual crossroads of a nation that is earnestly seeking to restore community values. I believe that in the future small churches will become anchor points for local pride and neighborhood identity. They will expand their important task of dispensing social outreach and spiritual comfort to the most marginalized of our society. They will witness to Christ with a language that speaks heart to heart.

This book begins with some generalizations about small churches and how they currently relate to their larger cousins and the denominational hierarchy above them. I believe that it is safe to say that an era of peaceful co-existence has now come to an end and that many small membership church leaders, both lay and clergy, feel themselves ostracized by their colleagues.

The first part of the book analyzes this "large versus small" thinking and also shows where and how bridges can be built. I believe that it is now important for congregations to overcome barriers of size, just as in the previous century they overcame inter-faith and denominational barriers, in order to form healthy cooperative relationships in every community. This section will also show how having congregations in a variety of sizes strengthens the ability of the greater church to reach the next generation for Christ.

The middle part of the book will present a middle way between stagnation and growth, a pathway on which a church of modest means and attendance can rediscover its purpose for being. Rather than advocating a new program or a simplistic cure for what ails the small church, this section will focus on what keeps a congregation healthy and equips her to fulfill her mission. The dead ends and dangerous curves of today's landscape will also be illuminated.

The book concludes with hopes for the future, as well as advice for making any church more accepting of change. In nature, small organisms are often highly adaptable and tenacious about doing what needs to be done to survive. The church, no matter the size, is not known for flexibility. Tradition may keep the fiddler on the roof, but if stubbornly held, tradition will also keep the next generation from our doors.

Much of what is presented at the beginning of the book, then, lays the foundation for the practical models and prescriptions for the changes that appear later. All of this unfolds from this insight that came to me when I returned to serve a small church after serving larger congregations for a dozen years. The people at Bairdford were intuitively discovering a middle pathway that enabled them to be both true to their faith and open to the needs of the community around them. The simple fashion in which they did church recalled me to the loving basics, which all fellowships need to do well if they are going to be vital and strong. I am profoundly grateful for this humbling lesson.

1 United Methodist figures based upon from General Board of Global Ministries Statistics (2002 records). For other denominations, see *Small Congregation Big Potential: Ministry in the Small Membership Church* by Lyle E. Schaller, Abingdon Press, 2003, page 209.

2 General Board of Global Ministries data compiled by John Southwick and published on GBGM web-page.

CHAPTER ONE

IMAGINE A PLACE

Imagine a countryside dotted with villages, towns, and cities, much like the American landscape. In this country a form of amnesia has taken hold of the political process: People assume that it is no longer possible to provide sustainable, vital, local government to small communities. If a village is too small to afford its own mayor, the populace becomes worried. "How shall we live without our own mayor?" Further, those in higher office, from the King on down, made speeches extolling the beauty and vitality of great cities. If a town is not on its way towards becoming a big city, then something must be wrong with it.

In this mythical land, people assume that once the current generation passes, village life will be gone forever. A few crossroad boroughs may survive as tourist stops, but no one would want to live in such small communities. Furthermore, young people entering careers in public service see the town and the country jobs as stepping stones to be endured before moving to higher positions. This stigma against small communities has become so embedded that no one seriously questions its logic, in spite of the fact that the majority of organized communities of this utopia are small—mere villages of a few dozen families.

This imaginary place mirrors the political geography of nearly every mainline denomination in America today. We live in a countryside dotted with small-membership congregations and yet, we fail to recognize their achievements or legitimize their natural wisdom for self organization. We have also succumbed to an amnesia that prevents us from accepting smaller congregations on their own terms.

And yet, remember these: The apostle Paul sent each of his epistles to small membership churches. Small monastic fellowships preserved the concepts of Christian discipleship and piety through the spiritual darkness of the Middle Ages. Brother Francis of Assisi's first act of obedience to the Lordship of Christ was to find an abandoned small church and work to reopen it for ministry. A small membership church in Montgomery, Alabama contributed its pastor, Dr. Martin Luther King, Jr., its prayers, and the courage of its laity, to the civil rights movement. Small membership churches continue not only to survive, but to contribute significantly to the health of our society.

Today many people assume that churches with less than 100 in worship are stubborn, backward, and unsustainable. Laity and clergy from larger congregations ask in wonderment, "How can a church be a real church if it can't afford to hire its own full-time pastor?" Current economic pressures, especially the rising cost of healthcare, put an impossible strain on those small membership churches that try to hold on to their own pastor. When a congregation accepts the new reality and seeks to transition to a part-time clergy or shared ministry arraignment, they rarely get the encouragement or guidance from their denominational leadership which they need.

Unrealistic expectations, both from the denominational leaders and from society, are plunging small membership churches into crisis, which is exacerbated by the rigidity of structures and lack of resources. This neglect is neither premeditated nor the responsibility of any individual or group. It is the product of a post-World War Two culture that valued bigger, faster, and richer over the simpler, more personal, expressions of faith found in the small membership church. The way our social value system has altered our perception of the small church needs further discussion, both here, and in the church at large.

Living by Different Rules

Consider the contrasts in the following list of organizational values:

Modern Cultural Value	Small Church Value
High value on accomplishing tasks.	High value on relationships.
Bullish attitude that seeks growth on every investment.	Bearish attitude that seeks to guard what has been entrusted to them.
Universal, "works everywhere," solutions to problems.	Context-sensitive solutions: "We have our way."
Think globally.	Focus locally.
Dynamic, highly flexible, organizational structures	Stable, change resistant, organizational structures
A process that first formulate goals and then evaluates progress	A process that emphasizes being faithful to fundamental habits
Future orientation!	Remember the past!
Focus on general principles and stated theology.	Focus on personal experience and individual faith.

Keep the right-hand listing of small church values in mind. They reveal the strengths and weaknesses and also allow us to predict what will and will not work for the small congregation. For now, it is important to see that neither set of values is necessarily "right" nor can the proponents of either column claim to be living a more faithful lifestyle. To adopt the left-hand column without theological reflection would be an impulsive sellout to contemporary pressures. To hold fast to the right-hand column purely for the sake of tradition would deny the world in which we currently live. And yet in each row, the values are mutually exclusive, challenging anyone to straddle the columns and find middle ground. Clearly a diversity of church structures and organizations are needed.

Churches that are intentionally seeking to grow need to forsake the traditional right column and vigorously shift left in all of their attitudes. This concept was first illuminated in the 1970's by early church growth authors such as Donald McGavran, C. Peter Wagner, Win Arn, and now is borne out in the professed culture of growing churches, such as Willow Creek, Saddleback, and Ginghamsburg churches. Adopting the left column is the unquestioned strategy for churches seeking to transition out of small-ness. Churches that weather the trauma of making this shift, soon cease to feel "small," no matter what their current attendance figures show (see the example of Faith Church in Chapter 3). Churches that drift from the left column towards the right simply stagnate and die.

Conversely, appreciating and being comfortable with the values in the right-hand column is the key to being happy as a leader or member of a congregation that is at home with "small-ness." This is the essence of what I describe as the "middle way" of congregational life. Among long-time small church members there is an almost Zen-like acceptance of the importance of just being. The church is what it is. It doesn't need to survey the community to discover its purpose or to bring in a church growth consultant in order to establish congregational objectives. A communal simplicity of purpose leaves people reticent to set goals and resistant to the work of clergy who want to see the kind of statistical growth which looks good on a resume. As the psalmist wrote, such churches are:

> "...like a tree planted by streams of water, which yields its fruit in season..."
> Psalm 1:3 NIV

Pastors and denominational leaders who have bought into the Modern Cultural attitude of the left column find this opposing small church mind-set mystifying, frustrating, and unquestionably wrong. They tell battle stories of how the laity sabotaged meetings held to formulate long term goals. The synod or conference programming staff wonder how these small church folk can remain so provincially-minded and oblivious to global concerns. The bishop groans as she receives yet another request from a small church for an inexpensive pastor who will "stay with us." In denominational gatherings, we speak in ways that denigrate the wisdom that forms the core values of small membership churches.

Far more than we care to admit, secular values have infiltrated the body politic of the church. This is not necessarily a bad thing. The church must constantly adapt to its internal structure and process to match the surrounding culture. When in Rome, we must do as the Romans do, so that we can be in a position to witness to them about Christ. Making our worship and our structures more "seeker friendly" has been a major task for the aging mainline denominations. But our commitment to this new way of thinking has become so all-consuming that it has blinded us to alternative viewpoints.

To understand the small church, one must grasp the concept that effective Christian witness can be made counter-culturally. How the small membership church does things, as well as what it values, sounds an intriguing note to those who are wearied by the speed, wastefulness, and material focus of today's society. Being locally focused, the small church reaffirms our inner longing for community. Being change-resistant, the small church provides a sense of stability to people feeling awash in social upheaval. Being focused on personal experience and individual faith, the small membership church reintroduces the people of our world to the intimacy that marked the relationships Jesus had with the people of Galilee.

We need to respect both voices, both value sets, in our dialogue about the church's future. The people of our land are reeling from global terror threats, mass marketing, and the multitude of impersonal intrusions fostered by today's information rich society. They are turning their attention to smaller fellowship settings that can meet their need for community. This changing tide of sentiment was aptly expressed in the theme song of the television comedy "Cheers," with the words, "You want to go where everybody knows your name."[1]

David's Paradigm

The lay leadership of small churches can often identify with the story of David trying on the armor of Saul before he went out to face the Philistine, Goliath. Not only do the resources sent from denominational offices often fail to fit the "boy-sized" congregation, but the weight of larger scaled expectations hinders their agility. Denominational officers, with their large congregation expectations, often fail to notice or reward the creative attempts of smaller churches to minister in their own context.

Remember how Saul and his officers assumed that one needed heavy armor to do battle? David instituted a paradigm shift for them in explaining how slingshots and light clothing fit the needs of shepherd boys doing battle against lions and bears, and perhaps even giants. In the same way denominational leadership, which is predominantly clergy, assumes that the minimum structure for a church involves at least one fully trained and ordained resident clergy for each worship location. This expectation weighs heavily on small congregations.

For the small church, being the minister is primarily a personal role, not an occupational task. The fact that the person who is their pastor may be part-time or have another secular job doesn't affect the personal role, which makes or breaks their pastor-parish relationship. This personal role is not enhanced by the successful completion of seminary or ordination. That I know this person and can trust them is the sole criteria. The vacant pulpits of many small churches are crying out for the lightly armored David of a pastor, who will spend his or her time meeting the needs of parishioners.

Not the Small Church's Problem

In every denomination there are leaders, whether known as Presbyters, Synod Presidents, Bishops, or District Superintendents, who spend their waking hours fretting over the retirement bubble, the rising cost of clergy compensation, and the decline in new seminarians. For those obsessed with the intricacies of clergy supply to see the small membership church as an asset to the denomination requires a great paradigm shift. What needs to be said in denominational centers is that these problems, however serious, are not the small membership church's problem.

Most mainline denominations are now reaping what they have sown. Over the last century much of the organizational focus has been on the role, quality, and rights of the ordained pastor. Even when we enter into important social debate on current issues such as homosexuality, our denominational time and energy is consumed by the question of who can be ordained. This is not the small church membership's question. Instead they ask, "What is the denomination doing so that we can continue to meet week by week on our little corner and learn about the life Jesus calls us to live?" This far simpler attitude deals with the important social issues on the intimate level of how the members plan to relate to the gay people that they know in their families and in the workplace.

Because they are so fixated on the who, what, and why of ordination, denominational leaders rarely build much trust among the laity of small membership churches. There is among the elderly a fading memory of a time in which denominational events would gather the laity from different sized churches together to hear the leadership preach the Gospel or address significant social issues. There remains a hope among many congregants that the organized church will shift its focus from institutional issues to address again matters of faith. The people of the small David-sized church desire to be challenged. They come to the cultural battlefront asking to do something more than simply provide lunch for the clergy. This frustration of the laity is often misunderstood, or worse, allowed to fester into anger and schismatic movements.

Many small membership churches have grown so weary of the party line that they seek for ways to leave the larger denomination. They say, "Wouldn't we better off on our own? We could get our neighbor, so and so, to preach." To think that this complaint is only about money misunderstands the underlying value set of the small church. Small churches would gladly pay denominational askings if the people saw the connection between this money and the effectiveness of their church. The same small churches that fail to pay the apportioned amounts to their judicatory contribute generously to non-denominational missionaries and local service projects. Their shift in loyalty again reflects their question, "What should we give as people, who because of this little church, are learning to live the life Jesus calls us to live?"

In some places, denominational leaders have successfully sowed the understanding that every worshiping congregation needs to have its own ordained full-time pastor. Because of issues that will be dealt with throughout the remainder of this book, financial resources have been falling behind inflation for the average small church for the last thirty years. Meanwhile, the cost of clergy compensation has risen dramatically, leaving many congregations to feel betrayed as they can no longer afford the clergy they have been so vigorously told they need.

Any gardener will tell you to not fertilize the things you don't want to grow. Sometimes denominational leaders will urge a struggling church to dig deep and take on an ordained clergy, whom they can not afford, by telling them that this person has the skills to make them grow. This effort both cultivates false hope and aims at a harvest that small church members may not be interested in consuming. The small church is interested in someone who will stay with them and live out the Gospel. They know that if this new pastor is such "hot stuff," he or she will soon leave them for greener pastures. They also are wise enough to know that real church growth is an organic process requiring change from within the congregation. Once away from the persuasive denominational leader, they recognize that expecting an outsider to make them grow is nothing but additional fertilizer raining down on them from above.

The clergy who has been encouraged to go somewhere for a lower salary because "the people will pay you more once they get to know you" are also set up for a fall. The root issue of the gap between fair compensation for highly trained professionals and the resources available to a small congregation needs to be addressed. I know of no example where a clergy has gone to a small membership church at a less than desirable salary and then in a reasonable time, has raised the compensation to a satisfactory level.

The clergy, denominational leadership, and the small membership congregations need to take a sobering look at the current religious context of our country and not take the situation so personally. Recent statistical research by Richard P. Deitzler has shown that substantial membership growth is now rarely occurring in churches averaging less than 500 in attendance.[3] Meanwhile, the cost of clergy compensation continues to rise. All of the factors driving up clergy compensation lie outside our control. There is nothing denominations can do to make ordained clergy affordable at one pastor to a church. A small church can do little to keep up with the rising cost of seminary trained pastors.

In my own denomination this problem is exasperated by rules that require a place to be found for every ordained pastor to serve. Not realizing that the new millennium would be one where very few clergy would be serving the traditional "single-point charge," the leadership has been caught with a threefold dilemma. Too many clergy are trained for and only happy in the vanishing one church-one pastor model. Too few laity are cultivated and trained for new roles in pastoral leadership now opening up in small churches. There are promises we cannot keep. But here again, small church people need to remind the denomination that this is not solely their problem.

Other Solutions

Returning to the question, "What can be done so that small congregations can continue to meet week by week to learn about the life Jesus calls them to live?" leads to many creative solutions to the problem of pastoral supply. Some churches are now forming partnerships to share a variety of Christian professionals, which include both lay and ordained ministers. The word "pastor" is being broadened to include anyone who performs a shepherding function within the life of the local church. Recognizing that life-experience may replace seminary training in qualifying a person to lead a congregation may be a stumbling block for some, but it rings true among those ascribing to small church values.

Small membership churches are also very adept at developing working ecumenical partnerships with neighboring congregations when they are encouraged to do so by their denomination. The members of a small United Methodist congregation may look across the street and notice that their friends at the Presbyterian church have been without a minister for over a year. Because they have done Vacation Bible School and Lenten services together, they already have some shared experiences. The way has been paved for sharing their pastor and thus reducing their clergy compensation costs. Both churches increase their own chances of survival, while at the same time create a partnership that may generate new programs to benefit the community.

Where "top-down" ecumenical efforts on the denominational level often fail to gain momentum and get bogged down in theological dialogue and questions of structure, two neighboring small churches can form a bridge based upon their mutual interests and mission to the community. Local church leaders usually have the skill and creativity to craft these partnerships so that what was distinctive about the two traditions is remembered and preserved. Membership roles may be kept separate, the calling of clergy alternated between the two denominations, and components of each church's liturgy incorporated into the weekly worship. Because the focus of the laity as they meet together is on the practical matters of what will work in this place, they often lay upon the table solutions that their judicatory officials would never dream of.

Another approach to the small church's financial problem lies in sharing building space or clergy time with outside programs and mission work. Thus the church's building serves the community as the home to a preschool, an AA group, or as the office for a non-profit agency while the church's pastor is part-time shepherd for the congregation and part-time administrator for some other entity. There are pitfalls to the landlording approach to balancing the church budget, and care must be taken to link the church's vision and mission with the work of any group that uses its facility. Once the small membership church stops thinking in terms of having an exclusive relationship with its pastor or building, new doors are opened for outreach. Sharing the pastor's time with other entities increases the churches visibility in the community. It also places the laity and clergy on more equal footing, each having some work-a-day experience of life outside the local church.

Diversity and the Barbie Doll Pyramid

Mattel Toys discovered that it could make huge profits from their Barbie doll line, even though most of these dolls were sold at a price point only marginally above Mattel's production costs. While competitors were making dolls priced between $15 and $20, the Barbie was a hit at $9.99. Mattel quickly achieved what business analysts call a dominant position, or "market share" of the low end doll market. This is a hard position to hold. Small changes in the costs of materials or labor can jeopardize one's ability to be competitive, and even if one is successful, the profits are meager. But holding onto the bottom tier of the market was a key component of a larger strategy envisioned by the executives at Mattel.[4]

In the formative years of our country, many denominations developed strategies for establishing congregations wherever there were people, even in the remotest frontier villages. The predecessors of the United Methodist Church placed these small fellowships on large circuits, in which lay people were trained to lead the fellowship in between the infrequent visits of ordained clergy. This system allowed each congregation to grow at its own speed. It was known from the start that not every location would grow large enough to support their own pastor. Like Mattel's Barbie, these locations remained at the low end of the religious market, serving a vital position in the denomination's total strategy. The strength of the Methodist tradition and its market share (now third among Protestant denominations) rests on a foundation of small congregations.

The sheer size of this base deserves restatement: 78% of all United Methodist Churches average 125 in weekly attendance or less. These 28,000 small churches, along with nearly 200,000 other small Protestant congregations, exist because they are meeting a need in the religious life or our country.[5] While small membership churches are numerous and pervasive in the American landscape, they have a limited capacity for attracting new members, meeting the needs of un-churched seekers, developing programming, and meeting some of the statistical expectations valued by denominational leaders. Like Mattel, we have discovered that the low end of the market is not the place to go for high profits.

Mattel's larger strategy is based on building a pyramid of products on the foundation of the low-priced Barbie. The next level on this doll pyramid is a sizable offering of accessories, specialty Barbie Dolls, and Barbie spin-offs, such as Midge and Ken. The profit margins are much higher on these products because the customer has already been hooked into the brand.

These Mattel products parallel the mid-sized program churches, which range between 125 to 350 people in weekly worship attendance. While numerous, and considered the mainstay of most denominations, they number less than 75,000 (23%) of the 325,000 Protestant churches in America. Small membership churches out number the "normal" sized churches 3:1. Mid-sized churches, however, have more say in denominational politics than the small churches because they do the things that denominations measure. They add new members each year, baptize children, offer various programs, pay denominational askings, and most important, manage to pay for their own ordained pastor.

For the United Methodist Church, whose polity has denominational leaders (bishop and cabinet) assigning (appointing) pastors to the local churches, one inadvertent tendency places the few remaining "traditional" clergy into these middle-sized churches. The middle-sized church provides one suitably average parsonage and has a seemingly standard work-load expectation suitable to one full-time clergy of the expected race, gender, age, and ethnicity. Clergy who are entering ministry as a second career, are half of a clergy couple, have specialized requirements due to family obligations or disability, or are in other ways "a hard sell," tend to be placed in the less standardized (more flexible) appointments found in small and large churches.

Many traditionally minded bishops and district superintendents find themselves perplexed by the way our modern era of diversity has stratified clergy and parish needs with a gaping hole where the middle used to be. The clergy placement process lacks both "standardized" people who can climb the ladder, as well as a large number of mid-sized congregations to form the middle rungs of the ladder. No longer does a young clergyperson graduate from seminary, enter a small church, and serve a progression of larger and more prestigious appointments until retirement at sixty-five from a downtown "First" church or denominational post. Today a person is more likely to enter the ministry following an early retirement from the military, the business arena, or teaching. They may come owning a house, which they are reluctant to leave. Many of them enter already disillusioned by experiences with corporate politics and the promises that precede a reassignment. They are unlikely to welcome a move from one church to another for the sake of a promotion. All they want is to settle down and do the Lord's work, preferably in a location that can accommodate their spouse's employment and is near enough for them to care for their elderly parents. Further, today's "average" pastor may be a foreign national, part of a clergy couple, or effectively serving in spite of what would previously have been considered a disabling condition.

For many pastors the movement from small church to mid-sized to large is impossible or undesirable. Churches and denominational officials who understand this now have the opportunity to negotiate flexible compensation packages with the individual clergy's needs in mind. The small church should no longer resign itself to losing their competent clergy for greener pastures. The best pastors may be happily kept if the church learns how it can creatively support their pastor's professional goals and family needs. This does not mean that the small church holds unrealistic expectations. They still will not be able to get qualified people to serve them for a pittance. But in matters such as housing and benefits, the small church can offer incentives and tailor compensation packages, which make them attractive to clergy with particular interests. For example, churches near recreational areas frequently seek ways to add skiing, golfing, or hunting perks to their church profile.

The place where this concept of the mid-sized church being the standard or normal church is most obvious in the matter of clergy housing. Both small and large churches can benefit in offering something different from the norm. Being more flexible about housing allows them to cater to individual diversity. In the United Methodist Church, which is highly invested in a system that provides housing, churches are usually expected to offer and maintain a parsonage within standard guidelines. District superintendents often prevent small churches from getting rid of their parsonage because the availability of housing keeps the church as a standard rung on the clergy career ladder. The mid-size church, which knows it has a high likelihood of receiving at the next pastoral change a clergy whose family situation is "traditional," does well to hold on to its parsonage, provided it meets all of the requirements of the denominational parsonage guide. The small church, however, because it is frequently served either by second career or bi-vocational clergy who own their own homes, finds itself in the position of renting out its parsonage while their current clergy lives elsewhere. This becomes a burden to the trustees and is rarely profitable. In the United Methodist system, rental lease agreements must be less than a year and end in May, so that the parsonage can be available if there should be a change of appointment. Worse still, the small church may find itself yoked together with another church that owns a parsonage, and where the new pastor will live becomes one of a dozen issues to resolve quickly. Often the first thing a small church congregation learns about their new pastor is that he or she does not want to live in the church-owned house. Chapter six returns to the question of how parsonage ownership affects a small church's chances for surviving through difficult times and how to develop meaningful partnerships with other congregations.

Mid-sized churches play the role of the norm in the denomination. Because they are in the middle of the Barbie-doll pyramid, the system assumes that what works for mid-sized churches should work for churches both larger and smaller. This is a false assumption. In subtle ways, however, the success of mid-size churches rests upon the foundation of smaller churches. I spoke with an active layperson and organist of a 400-member church that averaged just shy of 200 in worship. He waxed eloquently about his childhood in a small country church of 50 souls, a community which valued every person's talent and participation. He learned tithing and Bible stories in this intimate context of relatives and life-long friends. The nurturing influence of that two-room church has traveled with him and now sets the standard for his current participation in a mid-sized church.

Small membership churches serve as the training ground for entry level pastors, and they also contribute a disproportionate number of their own people into Christian service. My own story provides a counter example. I grew up in a large church. Even though I was an active, vocal member of the youth group, I was never asked to consider a career in Christian service. During my college years, as I attended and participated in a small membership church, I was challenged to put my talents and enthusiasm into serving the Lord.

To make a sweeping generalization, people who participate in mid-sized churches and some mainstream larger congregations see ministry as something done for them by trained professional clergy, who come to them from somewhere else. In the intimate setting of the small church, ministry is something which we all must participate in, and those who have special gifts and talents are obligated to hold their lamps up high. To hide gifts under a bushel basket is considered a mortal sin in the small congregation, which is operating so close to the margin of survival. This healthy attitude is carried up through the pyramid of churches by both clergy and laity as they transfer to larger congregations.

The Barbie doll pyramid also has a very small high-end product set where the profits are enormous. Nostalgic adults pay upwards of $250 for classic collector Barbie doll sets. This final level of the pyramid parallels the very large churches of our land. In megachurches, churches with over a thousand people in weekly attendance, the church growth statistics are spectacular. They are reaching the un-churched, adding new members, and funding multi-million dollar building and mission projects. Their senior pastors give keynote speeches at clergy conferences. They may count as personal acquaintances political leaders and social icons. They maintain the last vestige of Christian influence on secular power brokers. Note the size of this pyramid's top. About 25,000 (8%) of all Protestant churches average an attendance of more than 350, and of these, only 7,000 (2%) are truly very large, with worship attendance figures of more than 800. Even though large churches stand alone in gathering new members, none of the mainline denominations have been very successful in increasing the number of large churches in their fold.

Several things need to be said about large churches:

First, large churches cannot exist everywhere as small churches can. Large churches depend upon a sizable population from which to draw and a long-term relationship with a visionary senior pastor. The leadership gifts of the senior pastor, and his or her lay support team prove hard to find and even harder to reproduce or plant into other churches. Individuals who can successfully pastor a megachurch are as rare as winning NFL Quarterbacks or best-selling novelists. Few people have the mixture of evangelistic passion, intuitive organizational instincts, and people skills which mark a Bill Hybels (Willow Creek Church), a Rick Warren (Saddleback Church), or a John Ed Matheson (Frazer Memorial United Methodist Church).

Second, they rarely become large by following denominational policy. When a church is about to become a large church, it often drops the denominational logo from the marquee.

Third, large churches need to structure themselves like an association of small congregations in order to remain vital and be true to the gospel. Almost without exception, the megachurches have some type of small group ministry program or cell structure in place. They encourage and often require their members to participate in groups of a dozen or less individuals, so that every person will feel connected. The day is long gone and may never return when a church could stay large by being the platform for an exceptional preacher such as the relationship between Harry Emerson Fosdick and the Riverside Church. Today large churches must invent a special form of programming which imitates the routine experience of people who participate in a small membership church. They stay large by feeling small.

Fourth, while most large churches are on the conservative or evangelical end of the theological spectrum, becoming less liberal is not the pathway to growth. The key to growth is passion, and having clear core values that the whole congregation can state and become excited about. Large churches such as Glide Memorial United Methodist in San Francisco, California have grown strong while being consistent to their socially liberal witness. Small membership churches should not assume that their theology is keeping them small; they may instead need to examine whether or not the congregation can ever become passionate about what the church is currently stating as its beliefs. To have core values that the rank and file member can understand and state and feel comfortable sharing with their neighbors is more important to a small church that hopes to grow than to have beliefs that lean toward one end or the other of the theological spectrum.

Business analyst Jim Collins in his book *Built to Last* notes the correlation between having clear core values and being a successful and long lasting business. He argues that it is not important that a business have any particular set of core values—they can be hedonistic or humanitarian values. A great company simply needs values, any values will do, and those values need to be passionately and consistently communicated to their employees.[6]

The large church can never travel too far from the culture of the small membership church. Those of us who love the small church realize that we are not in competition with large churches. In fact, having a large church in one's neighborhood may be a plus for a small church. The flow of people back and forth between the two fertilizes and blesses each. Those who leave the small church carry with them a remembrance of its nurturing embrace. Those who return remind the small church culture that the Jesus' words still have relevance to our modern society. The wise small church leader seeks to understand "church growth values" even though they are not the values his or her fellowship connects with.

Here, for example, is the United Methodist pyramid: {figure 1.1}

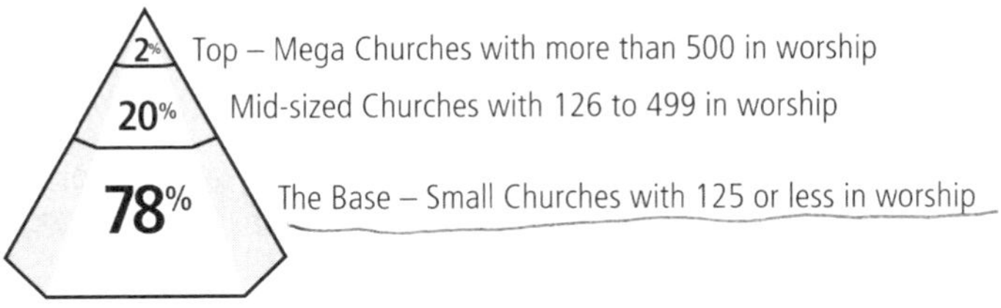

The Lesson

The lesson of the Barbie Doll pyramid is that a range of churches from very small to very large will be more successful in fulfilling the mission of Christ, than a homogenous denomination in which every church is the same size. In fact there may be some yet-to-be-understood sociological underpinning to the proportions of the church size pyramid. As people seek to join fellowships of faith, one size does not fit all. Those who do not find a church of a size they find comfortable may fail to be incorporated into the organized church. Reducing the base of a pyramid always reduces the potential volume of the structure. If we lose our small church base, we might also lose our capacity to support an expanding mid-size and large church ministry.

The diversity inherent in smaller churches allows them to hollow out competitive niches for themselves in underserved aspects of the American religious market. Like lichen in the arctic tundra, small churches have the capacity to cling to life in hostile environment. Their size enables them to be locally focused and sensitive to the context of urban neighborhoods whose wealthy residents have fled to the suburbs. Their focus on relationships and stable, change-resistant organizational structures enable them to stay open in rural communities that have lost their young adults. This same diversity, however, means that the needs and vulnerabilities of small churches are rarely understood by the denominational hierarchy. Clergy who succeed in one small church setting may find themselves chewed up by the expectations of another. Furthermore, seminary graduates who have learned well the universal principles of church life that larger churches hold as a standard, will find themselves racing to re-learn the local, "this is the way we do things," adaptations of small church life.

For the last twenty-five years I have served as a pastor within a denomination that has a broad range of congregational sizes from the over 15,000 microchurches with 35 or less in attendance to a handful of megachurches which boast over 1,500 in worship.[7] Instead of celebrating this diversity, denominational leadership often expresses dismay that the smaller churches are not working effectively at becoming larger churches. Just as a shotgun with its scattering of small pellets has a greater chance of hitting a target, so casting churches of varied sizes out into the landscape increases the impact of a denomination. This wisdom is captured in the words:

> Cast your bread upon the waters, for after many days you will find it again.
>
> Give portions to seven, yes to eight, for you do not know what disaster may come upon the land.
>
> Ecclesiastes 11:1-2

Let the Lower Lights Be Burning

When the next generation goes seeking for a more intimate worship experience, will there still be "the little brown church in the vale?" If the small church were to disappear in the decades ahead and its steeples no longer influence our

American landscape, I believe that the loss would be felt by the various Protestant denominations to which these churches belong and also mourned deeply by our society. Small churches are particularly important in two settings.

The first is out in the crossroads, where a single small church may be the only Christian witness to a particular community of people. The advent of the automobile has greatly broadened the range that the average family will roam for worship and other social needs. Many people today drive twenty miles one-way to church. This has been a boom to large and mid-size churches, which are able to gear their message and ministries to attract people from across a metro region. This trend hides the great affinity many Americans feel for their immediate neighborhood. The greatest strength of small membership churches is their ability to be scaled back in size to fit in near to where people live.

Neighborhood churches provide the only available corporate worship to people with limited transportation—the old, the young, and the economically challenged. Small churches also are the logical fit for people who have chosen to live in this neighborhood because it is a retreat from the crowds of the city. Further, there is a deep sense of identification between home and sanctuary that resonates in the hearts of many, perhaps most, Americans. When denominational officials urge the people of one rural crossroad to give up their church and travel down the road to the next town, they need to first root themselves in the experience of the individuals involved.

Many small churches are the last institution for which there is any sense of local identity. They may sit at a rural junction that once hosted a mom-and-pop store, a Grange hall, a post office, a school, and three taverns. Today only the church and one bar remain, and the church is the only place with the village's name on its marquee.

Many social commentators speak about the need to maintain the "social capital" of our communities, by which they mean the volunteer investment families and individuals make back into the place where they live. If people have no personal stake in their home-base, whether it be a transitional inner city neighborhood, a comfortable suburb, or a rural crossroad, then the livability of the place will decline. If they simply pay taxes and maintain their house, but do not personally commit themselves by joining group ventures within their neighborhood, then democracy will be weakened and the pride in our country will be misplaced. The local volunteer groups to which we belong, especially the intimate, values-oriented ones like the small church, are the best investment accounts we have for our neighborhoods. They build a sense of local identity. They often house the food banks and economic ministries which minister to the needs of the poor and reconnect the disenfranchised. Because they meet weekly as a group and listen to the heroics of God's people in the Bible, small church members are natural instigators for change. The church is frequently the anonymous key donor and catalyst for the social projects that benefit everyone, and in the rural communities, the small country church may be the only organization left to fulfill this task.

Small churches are important to the fabric of our society is in the economically challenged urban neighborhoods and high density population areas. In providing an alternative or supplemental location for human services, such as ministries to the homeless, neighborhood watch groups, recovery groups, food and clothing distribution centers, the small membership church delivers goods and services from a faith perspective. By their very nature, secular and governmental human services reinforce the recipient's dependency, both by fostering an attitude of entitlement and by introducing them to an impersonal relationship with a bureaucracy. Secular groups are not permitted to supplement their charity with a hug or share the good news of how valuable the recipient is in the eyes of God. Further, they have little incentive to work against the root causes of poverty or to prophetically challenge the institutions that degrade the value of a neighborhood. In one urban area, small churches band together into a faith-based initiative to challenge the lending practices of banks which had "blue lined" certain neighborhoods making it hard to get home mortgages in these neighborhoods.

Here again, the small membership church ministers in a package that fits small, isolated communities. Often the focus of neighborhood ministry in an urban landscape will be only a few blocks long or is an ethnic community that needs transitional support. The people of a neighborhood's small church can notice holes in the social services net, holes that are too small to notice by those who write large grants and hire program administrators. Because it is their own neighborhood and their own project, the mission work of these small urban churches speak with great authenticity.

This brings us to one of the odd benefits of the church growth movement. In most metro areas across the country, growing congregations have fled the inner city and built large "campuses" (church complexes) in the suburbs. The relationally minded, "people-driven," small churches, though, remain fixed to the urban landscape. Whether they discern the call of God telling them to stay or because their sense of tradition prevents them from leaving their old stone building, these declining congregations inherit a deep responsibility for their neighborhoods. They can become critical lighthouses for Christian hope if they intentionally do two things: first adapt and become sensitive to the culture of the people who remain in and immigrate into the city; and second, form partnerships with the growing suburban churches who can provide additional resources for ministry.

The partnership of large church with small church can take various forms. A large church might adopt one or two small congregations as their mission outposts, funneling volunteers and resources to them. Alternatively the small worshiping congregation might find themselves part of a bigger mission umbrella, which sponsors a variety of programs to meet the needs of the community. The small church can quickly get to the point where its own identity and the identity of the mission group merge. Because small churches are by nature locally minded, context sensitive, and focused on the personal experience of providing hospitality to those in need, what we think of as "church;" that is, having a theological creed, a pastor, and a dedicated sanctuary, can become blurred and unrecognizable. I know of one small Lutheran church in a blighted inner city neighborhood that officially closed as a church because they could no longer call a pastor. But their food bank and soup kitchen remained open and successful. Neighboring clergy share preaching duties at a vibrant worship service before the meal. Resources and volunteers flow in from all over the city, and trained staff are available to provide counseling. The church is more of a church now than when it was officially a church.

In establishing relationships between large and small churches, both parties must guard against forming a co-dependent system. The large congregation must recognize the value set of the small church as separate but equal to its own organizational principles. Large church leadership may be prone to patronize the small congregation, giving un-requested advice or stepping into internal affairs. The small church also must understand that it exists by God's grace, not because of the good will of the church in the suburbs. They must see the resources that come to them from the large church not as charity or cast-offs, but as a recognition that the small church is serving on the front lines and has the personal distribution network to do what needs to be done. An interdependent relationship between small and large congregations needs to be intentionally formed where each party recognizes the others separateness and intrinsic worth. The small church is an important link in the giving chain; they link those in need with those who need to give.

Many small membership churches act as transitional communities serving the needs of those outside American mainstream. When Hispanic people immigrated into a small northeastern city, only a few of this group felt comfortable assimilating into an existing church. The large Catholic churches, which would have been the first choice of most of these individuals, barely noticed this influx. But several small churches—one Pentecostal, another United Methodist—quickly sprung up. In a similar way, the recent immigrants from the former Soviet Union, upon moving into this city have spawned several small churches along ethnic and theological lines, while only marginally contributing to the larger Eastern Orthodox congregations.

These small churches, while providing both fellowship and guidance for those whose native language is not English, show flexibility to meet the needs of current immigrants, whose culture may differ greatly even from previous immigrants from the same region. These little fellowships can spring up quickly from the grass roots, not waiting for the support or blessing of denominational church planters. None of these congregations has any hope of growing past their small church status, as the population they draw from is limited and transient. Allowing one of these small ethnic congregations to share their building is one way small mainstream congregations can enter into mission.

Small membership churches, whether they are on the crossroads of rural America or in the depressed neighborhoods of our cities fulfill by their active presence the call of the old gospel hymn which proclaimed:

> Brightly beams, our Father's mercy
> From His lighthouse evermore,
> But to us He gives the keeping
> Of the lights along the shore.
> Let the lower lights be burning!
> Send a gleam across the wave!
> Some poor fainting, struggling sea-man
> You may rescue, you may save.
> [P. P. Bliss]

1 Another presentation of these contrasting values is found in *Entering the World of the of the Small Church* by Anthony Pappas (Alban Institute, 2000).

2 Words by Gary Portnoy and Judy Hart Angelo.

3 *The Ice Cube is Melting* by Lyle Schaller (Abingdon Press, 2004)

4 A full account of the pyramid profit model employed by Mattel can be found in *The Art of Profitability* by Adrian Slywotsky, AOL Time Warner 2002).

5 *Small Congregation Big Potential, Ministry in the Small Membership Church* by Lyle E. Schaller (Abingdon Press, 2003) p. 24.

6 *Built to Last* by Jim C. Collins and Jerry I. Porrass (Harper Business, 1994) 6 pp. 47-79.

7 *Small Congregation Big Potential* by Lyle Schaller p. p. 207.

CHAPTER TWO

THE MIDDLE WAY

In Homer's *Odyssey*, Ulysses is forced to steer his craft between two dangers. On the one hand there was a six-headed monster threatening to devour his men, and on the other side there was a whirlpool waiting to swallow up any vessel that fled the monster. Every small church understands brave Ulysses' plight as they chart their course through these dangerous times.

Looming to one side are the multiple threats of modernity. A short list of the dangers that make up the snatching jaws of this monster would include:

> Large churches have so raised the expectations that people have for church programming that small churches can no longer compete. New residents in town bypass the small church to go where they can get the activities they want.
>
> The biblically illiterate, relativistic, new-age spirituality of today's culture is at odds with the small church's respect for traditional truths. What the church does in worship is not relevant.
>
> The financial investment needed for church growth, such as changes in facilities and staff, can quickly devour the resources of a small church. Every new pastor brings a different "sure fire" and expensive program for growing the church. The people are tired of investing the time and money and not getting the results.
>
> Failure to fill the pulpit with a qualified, but youth-oriented pastor of the expected gender and race, leads to the loss of members.
>
> As neighborhoods change, new highways either bypass the church or create such traffic difficulties that the small church is cut off from people. Parking is, for many, an unsolvable problem.
>
> The silent generation (those past retirement age) who sacrificed for the church and led with integrity are aging and dying. The current middle-aged generation (the baby boomers) seem reluctant to pick up the reigns of leadership. The old guard, who seemed to know instinctively how church should be done and had all the answers, is now being replaced by a generation that knows only the questions.

Ulysses, aware of the whirlpool, chose to steer nearer to the monster. This choice meant losing some beloved people to the monster. He was tempted to give up his voyage altogether. The small church constantly wonders if it is simply holding out against the inevitable. Should we cut our losses and close? Should we somehow join the monster and become a church with an entirely contemporary value set and mission? Most small churches respond to these challenges reactively. They push their tiller hard, over steering their course straight into the whirlpool.

The whirlpool symbolizes the opposing problem of stagnation and apathy. If the church fails to do some new things, it will die. If it allows its vitality to be sucked up by a parochial vision and a "stuck in the mud" attitude, no future generation will receive what the small church has preserved. Each of the monstrous problems listed above are opportunities for the church to re-examine its historic truth. We should not flee from the challenges of living in today's world.

How would Jesus steer the church today? I do not think he would agree with those who see the small traditional churches as endangered by large church values. For Jesus, each church, no matter how small, is a place where his saving grace is offered, his body sacramentally shared, his word taught, and his presence experienced. He would have us focus on these things. Modern versus traditional, small versus large church distinctions blur the deeper truth that differing churches carry the same grace to a broken world. I don't think Jesus would tell any congregation to give up because they are losing members to other churches or failing to attract younger families.

For Jesus, the kingdom of God is like a sower sowing seed (Matthew 13:3-9). The seed cannot choose where it is planted, anymore than a church can choose its social context, but each seed must make its own best attempt to grow where it is planted. While the results in terms of numbers will be different for different seeds and their soils, each seed that does produce fruit will testify to God's power and love. So whether the current attendance is thirty, sixty, or a hundred, the church's reason for existing relates to God's plan for producing fruit throughout the earth. Each church is a miracle of God's power.

Some churches need to accept the limitations imposed by their situation. This is, however, not an excuse for mediocrity. Creativity and passionate spirituality need to be cultivated no matter how small the church. To tolerate low standards and pettiness of vision is to steer a church, no matter how rich its tradition, into the whirlpool. Just as water circles down the drain, so many churches, both large and small, have turned inward in their aspirations. They are satisfied to meet the needs of their membership only and fail to wrestle with the monstrous reality of a world that needs their bold witness to faith.

This chapter develops a concept I call the "middle way." Even small churches can chart a course that confronts all the issues of modernity without being consumed. Two principles form this middle way: scalability, which relates to the flow of energy in the church, and simplicity, which relates to the flow of love. Think of a car driven down a road. Scalability refers to the use of the gas and brake pedals. A safe driver must scale his or her speed to match the conditions of the road. Simplicity relates to the steering wheel. It asks, "Where will we direct our vehicle? Who are "our kind of people"? What is our mission and/or destination?"

Scalability

Vital, healthy, and sustainable church fellowships come in all sizes. If a church has a problem being vital, or paying its bills, or keeping open for the future, the solution does not lie in growing. More people will not solve any of a small church's problems. In fact when we try to bring people in because we think they will help us meet expenses or "liven the place up," we drive them away. The corollary to this truth is that the growing small churches are the ones that have discovered the middle way of contentment with who they currently are, and so are winsomely attracting people who notice the church's vitality, health, and long-term security.

Scalability is so counter-intuitive that it needs some explanation. Like the nature of life on earth itself, Christian fellowship and worship can adapt itself to any environment. The church can be small where it needs to be small. A few inmates meeting in a corner of the prison yard, a dozen migrant workers in a farmhouse, a busload of travelers on their way to see the Holy Land, can all constitute "church." Jesus said, "where two or three come together in my name, there am I with them" (Matthew 18:20 NIV). Whenever institutions or social pressures seek to eliminate the bottom end of the scale of Christian fellowships or imply that a certain sized building or Sunday attendance is necessary for a congregation to be a "real" church, they are behaving in ways contrary to the organic activity of the Holy Spirit.

When Jesus uses the word "church" (Greek *"ekklésia"*), there is not a hint that he has a particular sized unit in mind (Matthew 16:18, 18:17; see also Revelation chapters 2 & 3). It is true that First Church Jerusalem was birthed as a megachurch of 3,000 members (Acts 2:41), but as evangelists and apostles fanned out into the Mediterranean world they formed fellowships in people's homes and considered these small groups to be "church." To me, history reveals how the Spirit of God seeks to create a form of religious life to fill every social niche. The range of church sizes we see in this country parallels the Darwinian principles of biodiversity, or as it was said in the movie *Jurassic Park*, "life always finds a way."

Because those who love and lead the church tend to focus on church buildings rather than church congregations, few people grasp this natural principle of scalability. Church buildings tend not to be easily scalable. They are difficult to adjust to current conditions. To return to the automotive metaphor, assuming that a congregation has to maintain a certain income or number of people in attendance because of its building is like setting the cruise control of your car to fifty-five and refusing to touch the brakes.

Each church building is designed for a certain number of worshipers. When fewer than that number gathers week after week, not only are resources wasted on utilities and maintenance, but the empty pew space also saps the congregation's vitality. Members look around and think that something must be wrong or people would fill the seats. Architectural features, such as a vaulted ceiling, might add to this sense that a congregation is lost in a space they no longer deserve to occupy. Smaller numbers also require more intimate expressions of worship. Pipe organs accentuate a feeling of distance whereas piano, acoustical guitar, or even an autoharp, might more successfully lead a small group into worship.

In another ancient Greek legend, the weary traveler Thesius encounters a madman named Procrustes who offers him a bed for the night. This was not a kindly offer, for Procrustes would size up his guests and if the person was too short for the bed, he would put the guest on the rack and stretch him to fit the bed. If the house guest was too tall for the bed, Procrustes would cut off the traveler's legs. This legend applies aptly to how congregations to adapt to their buildings. When we alter people to fit a material object, whether it be a bed or a hundred-year-old building, we are being, to use another Greek term, draconian. When a congregation does not lie comfortably within the designed space of its building, the first option should not be to trim or expand the congregation.

A modern architectural principle states that a building's form should follow from its function. The outward form of a small church often doesn't match the way the congregation functions. Thinking in terms of scalability, we look at our building and ask:

Is it too small?

Is there room for visitors to worship without sitting in the front seat?

If my parking space is taken, how easy is it to find another?

Is there room for us to gather for fellowship and group activities without having to move a lot of stuff?

Is there room for children to be children?

Or, is the building too large for the congregation?

Are there more than three seats sideways, or one pew front and back, between my family and the next one?

Is there an echo in here? Does worship feel cold?

Is most of our offering going to utilities and maintenance rather than to programs, missions, and pastoral leadership?

Some small congregations are small because they are living at the top range of their building's capacity. They may need to expand their parking or add a room so that the current congregation fits comfortably in the mid-range of their facility's capabilities. They may be pleasantly surprised by a growth in attendance. Even if they do not see growth, they will reside more in the middle of their structure's comfort range.

Some small congregations feel small and insignificant because they are living in a structure that is way too big. They may need to consider inviting another ministry or mission to share their space with them. Selling their current structure and moving into smaller quarters is a far less drastic solution than closing the church. It is surprising how many churches believe they are dying when they simply need to trim their structure.

To live in the middle way and adapt to their location, every small church must periodically take a sober look at their building. Churches should see their building the way a hermit crab sees its shell. The crab will not stay with a shell that forces unreasonable expectations of growth. The shell must fit or else the crab seeks a new shell. When the exterior form of a congregation's building matches the interior functions of the church's daily life, a beautiful thing occurs. The congregation settles into a groove. They feel a renewed freedom to worship. They creatively spawn new programs and freely drop old ineffective programs. What the church does throughout the week fits their space like fingers in a glove.

I became aware of this happy equilibrium while attending a trustee meeting at the Bairdford United Methodist Church. The people of Bairdford are, by and large, content within their small (2,200 square feet), eighty-year-old building. The small sanctuary and parking lot perfectly matches the fifty weekly worship attendees. Downstairs, three rooms and a kitchen provide sufficient space for various activities, including a very popular senior lunch program and some use by the outside community. Of course in this happy family there are periodic complaints; the fellowship hall maxes out at seating eighty people, the upstairs lacks a restroom, the office space is inadequate, and the whole building lacks accessibility. They are in the middle of their building's designed capacity, but the facility is far from perfect.

This trustee meeting began with a proposal to fix one of these space limitations. "Could we add on a little ten-by-ten room to provide a unisex bathroom near the sanctuary?" This comment led to other equally valid proposals to add a few hundred square feet here and there to meet the other needs. A similar addition in the lower level would surely improve the fellowship space. What about the office and the kitchen? Each proposal nibbled a little deeper into the church's limited parking area. Each square foot multiplied the costs of expansion and threatened to set into motion the local building codes and thereby raise further issues. Finally a trustee, who had been silent throughout the discussion, spoke up. "These things would be good to do because they would attract new people and help us to grow. But where will these new people park? Will these new people be ready to jump right in and help us to pay for all these improvements?"

As the meeting shifted back to its normal agenda, I gained a new appreciation of what it meant for these people to be the church in their own limited context. They were like a violet blooming vigorously in a tight pot. Suburban sprawl was bringing many new neighbors into their region, most of whom drove past this little white clapboard church seeking the programs and facilities offered by larger churches. If this little violet of a church traumatically re-potted itself, it could grow, and might in time learn how to bloom in a new context. But at this meeting, they did not feel led to make this transformation. Instead, they felt that God's call upon them was to be faithful in the current middle way, a path that led them between growth and stagnation.

Contrast this situation with another church in a different location facing the same issues. Hill Memorial also felt confined by inadequate restrooms, fellowship space, office location, and the lack of accessibility. In addition they felt a passion to reach out to the children and youth of the community. They envisioned programs that would feed the hungry, build community capital, and present the Gospel through contemporary Christian drama and music to unchurched people. They acted on this vision, recognizing that it would require great financial sacrifice and a total disruption of their current church life. They also decided not to pare back on the number of things they wanted to fix in this expansion; it was either do the whole laundry list or do nothing. Perhaps the greatest risk was the awareness that they would lose parking and would have to sacrifice again financially to buy adjacent land when the opportunity arose. There was nothing moderate about the path of growth on which they felt God had called them to run.

Both churches responded in faith and have done the right thing. But at the risk of second-guessing the will of God, what factors were different between the two situations? Hill was larger in terms of attendance, averaging about 150 in worship, but it was the same or smaller in terms of resources available to meet the project. The two were not different in terms of how much sacrifice would be required out of their members to do an expansion. What made the difference is that as a middle-sized church in the mid-range of the churches of its town, Hill needed to present quality programs in order to maintain vitality and attract new members. If Hill did not take the risk and re-pot itself so that it could reach out to the children and youth of the community, it would die. If the members did not have the facilities to feed the community or do musical productions, they would feel limited by their church building. Their hand needed a new glove.

Each church has a market related to the vision of its membership, and each church has a niche it must occupy in the context of the community in which it lives. Size matters in the sense that a congregation with the wrong sized building for its niche will struggle with feelings of inadequacy. The vision that a people have is like the mind within the human body. If the body is obese or malnourished, it will be hard to sustain an appearance of vitality or achieve greatness.

Clergy and denominational leadership often speak and act as if the goal is to increase the number of people worshiping per church building. This leads to sometimes harsh interventions, demanding that some churches build while disparaging any small churches which lack the potential or vision for growth. I, however, hear Jesus differently when he speaks of the goal of making disciples (Matthew 28:19-20). Disciples are to be made in every niche and context, and these disciples are to be taught how to use their faith reach both their immediate community and then the world. The goal then is the number of fully formed disciples per geographic region, instead of the number of people per church.

This being said, it is important to understand that having an idolatrous love for one's church building is a sin, and one of two surefire ways for a congregation to lose its vitality. The other disastrous idolatry happens when a congregation thinks that they cannot live without their current pastor. Both buildings and pastors are temporary vessels to be employed by a congregation for as long as they support the fellowship in performing her mission.

Programming in the Small Church

If the mission of a denomination is to make Christian disciples throughout a geographic region, then we must ask, "Are our structures scalable?" The word *structures* applies not just to buildings, but also to programs and administrative matters. Many small churches labor under the mistaken notion that they must do all the things that other "normal" churches do. They lack a guideline as to what is normal in the small church.

For the microchurch with thirty-five or less in attendance at worship, normal is:

- One weekly worship service
- One or two programs, study groups, or activities
- Not a separate children or youth ministry, but some attempt to include them with the adults. What we do for Christian education feels more like the old one-room schoolhouse.

No separate committee meetings, but decisions are made for the church in a regular monthly, or sometimes quarterly, meeting (church council), which all members are free to attend.

Very little formal administration or policies. Things get done around the church by volunteers.

For the small church with more than thirty-five in worship, normal is:

Some additional worship and study experiences beyond Sunday morning are added, especially around holidays, and done in rotation or cooperatively with other churches.

Three to five programs and activities now fill the church calendar

Children and/or youth may have a separate study or fellowship experience, but its size and shape will depend upon the number of families with kids.

In addition to the monthly board or council meetings (which are still open to everyone to attend), a committee looks after the building (trustees) and a committee relates to the pastor.

Most things get done by the women's group or by the men of the church. If something else needs to happen, a person will head a temporary committee. This committee may become permanent.

Communication works naturally in smaller scaled fellowships because everyone feels connected with someone else who is on the committee that is doing whatever needs to be done. When a church moves closer to a hundred in worship, a new structure becomes necessary. Now committees plan programs without knowing the church treasurer or having any relatives on the Trustees. They will need a more formal way to request resources or receive permission to act. In scaling the church structure to suit the congregation of a hundred or more attendees, the lay leadership, and not just the pastor, must read and understand those parts of the denomination's rule book that govern local church life. For this sized church, it is better to have too much administrative structure rather than too little. Communication is never as good as we imagine it. Often this sized church is rife with conflict and burned-out church workers because they lack functional programming structures.

My own denomination's rulebook (*The Book of Discipline*) has a number of places with language such as "every local church shall have..." As mentioned before, very few of the delegates who voted on this language are acquainted with small church life. Each small church must tailor its structures, that is, buildings, program, and committee meetings, to meet its current context. If small churches find that the organizational structures of the denomination do not work for them, then they should feel free to organize themselves in more locally minded way. The rules we live by and the meetings we hold must honor every person present and lovingly distribute the decision making process to empower everyone. In the small church, the wisdom to do this is to be found in prayer and intuitive listening, rather than by strict adherence to a rule book.

There are disciples to be made and nurtured at both ends of the church size scale. If we are not stimulating vital congregations right down to the level of a few dozen people, we are missing the opportunity to make disciples in many contexts of our culture. On the other hand, the denomination that fails to encourage the growth of megachurches or denies them the right to organize in creative ways to grow their ministry, will miss one of the richest opportunities for disciple-making in our time. My argument here is not just on behalf of the small membership church, but rather, to present scalability as a part of God's plan for the whole church. Local church life needs to be so equipped by its denomination that it feels *normal* no matter what the congregation's size.

Simplicity

Where scalability had to do with downsizing the buildings, programs, and committee work of the church so that there is sufficient energy available for the small congregation to be vital, simplicity has to do with steering the church towards the middle of its target audience and creating a stable environment for people to learn how to love one another. Small church members will express love most clearly when they have a simple and humble understanding of who they are and with whom God has called them to be in fellowship. This singleness of purpose marks many small membership churches today. The people of these churches can identify the cultural and physical boundaries of their parish and have little desire to travel outside their home base. They have learned the principle of simplicity.

Medium and large churches grow and maintain vitality by living out the Pauline motto of "*being all things to all people*" (I Corinthians 9:22). Here the apostle expresses a scattergun or broadcasting method for church growth. Paul had little interest in restricting his work to the tiny Jewish enclaves dotting the back alleys of the Roman Empire. He instead marched through Macedonia, setting his sights on Corinth, Athens, and Rome. Setting up his soapbox pulpit as near as he could to the crossroads of the culture, he became student of diverse languages and customs. He sought to incorporate as many people groups as possible into the body of Christ. This put Paul on a path of constant change. His personal values (like the left-hand column of the chart in chapter one) were task oriented, globally minded, and constantly looking to the future. He had a businesslike attitude towards maximizing the investment he made in each place. Paul was neither simple nor parochial. Megachurch pastors often share Paul's personality traits and passions. Having a pastor like Paul in the small church is as destructive as the proverbial bull in a china shop.

Congregations of more than a hundred in worship need to master the complex programming task of providing something for everyone. If they want growth and vitality, they cannot afford to be simple. One pastor described his church as a greenhouse, which nurtured diverse and sometimes contradictory groups of people. Each flowering species had its own pot, but all were under one roof. He was constantly seeking to add more small groups to this ministry because it was the only way to keep diverse people connected and related as the church grew. Another leader said that her church was, on its good days, like a three-ring circus. This ringmaster of a growing church was often near a panic because her congregational elephants threatened to step on her clowns, but she knew that this church needed to cultivate this creative chaos in order to keep the crowds coming.

When a large church ceases to accommodate diversity, it becomes cliquish and stagnates. When a medium-sized congregation is content with its current programs and fails to update its offerings to the community, it begins to die gradually. For congregations with more than 100 in worship, America's current religious audience is extremely fickle. They need clear road signs, ample parking, and a church staff that is creatively attempting to interest an ever widening circle of new prospects. This means that many formerly medium-sized congregations, as well as some recently large churches, are now sliding down the attendance scale and becoming small church sized. They now have the worst of both worlds: they do not know what it means to be simple, nor do they have the resources to be complex.

Because medium and large churches have this culture of complexity and spend so much energy at the task of accommodating everyone into their own structure, they are often reticent about forming partnerships with other churches. They want to keep their outside relationships trimmed down to something simple and manageable that will not interfere with their own expanding programs. This is why small churches often encounter difficulties when they turn to their larger church neighbors and attempt to develop cooperative ministries. Large churches operate by constantly incorporating small groups into their own internal structure. They usually lack a model for dealing with a small group, which wishes not to be assimilated, but rather to be respected and related to as an equal.

Small churches live in a different world. They can afford to be diverse in their external relationships because inside their walls they have a simple one-group fellowship. Instead of trying to provide something for everyone, they seek to get everyone to attend the same thing. Theirs is the motto of Thoreau who wrote, *"Our life is frittered away by detail... Simplicity, simplicity, simplicity! I say, let your affairs be as two or three, and not a hundred or a thousand... Simplify, simplify, simplify!"*[1] Small church leaders frankly recognize that they will not be able to accommodate everyone's divergent tastes under their tiny roof. They have chosen a simpler path, one that remains closer to Thoreau's humble dwelling at Walden Pond.

This simplicity can be both appealing and frightening to an outsider. Some people fleeing a hectic life may be pleasantly surprised to see only a few announcements listed in the weekly bulletin. It may take them a while, however, to get past the assumption that something must be wrong with a church that does so little. There is a casualness about the flow of worship, and time is provided to greet everyone, not just those who share the pew. Unlike the megachurch, the small church often has dead air time in its program. Unplanned interruptions must be hunted down and eliminated from the worship program of the larger church, but a small church freely allows and encourages the silence and the fidgeting of infants into its service. One of the smallest of the Psalms puts it this way:

> O Lord, my heart is not lifted up, my eyes are not raised too high;
>
> I do not occupy myself with things too great and too marvelous for me.
>
> But I have calmed and quieted my soul, like a weaned child with its mother;
>
> my soul is like the weaned child that is with me.
>
> (Psalm 131:1-2 NRSV)

The simplicity of a small church reinforces its sense of intimacy. Those in worship are not a crowd, but a collection of individuals. Members notice one another's quirks and mannerisms every Sunday. When one of them offends another, the small church does not provide the space to avoid them by sitting in a different section or attending a different service time. The small church has a simple "on the job training" approach to Jesus' command that we should love one another (John 13:34-35). Instead of presenting it as a theoretical concept, the small church presents this teaching as a way of life that challenges, exercises, and deepens each time the fellowship gathers.

Instead of feeling embarrassed because they lack sports programs and professional choirs, small churches should rejoice that their congregation's natural simplicity enables them to live Jesus' gospel more intuitively. People who gather in small churches can name the prodigal sons and daughters who have returned to the church's communal family. They personally know a widow who has given her last mite to repair the church roof and will talk about the good Samaritan who came in their need. They know the names of the children who played angels at the last Christmas play and the trustee who shovels the walk. They feel personally invited by the blessings that Jesus spoke to those who gathered on the Galilean hill long ago. They too are a few humble souls, poor in spirit, hearing the truth that, even in this little church, they are members of the kingdom of God. In their simplicity, they are the salt of the earth and the church a real house of prayer.

Simplicity, however, is not an excuse for mediocrity. When only a few people gather for worship, it is tempting for the pastor and other leaders to feel that what they do does not matter. Each worship service, however small, is an expression of our collective passion for and appreciation of God. Spiritual passion is an essential characteristic for all church leaders, laity as well as clergy, and the church that does not cultivate this has a serious difficulty. Apathy is a disease or curse unrelated to the size of a congregation.

By simplicity, I mean a clarity of vision and a willingness to let go of what is not essential in order to be true to this particular church's calling. Great painters often restrict themselves to a limited palette, as they strive to express the essence of beauty. Memorable music works because it uses a basic tonal scale with elegant simplicity. Remember what Jesus said to quell a conflict in the small fellowship which met at Bethany:

> "Martha, Martha, you are worried and distracted by many things; there is need of only one thing. Mary has chosen the better part [or the gift Jesus promises to the church – his presence], which will not be taken away from her."
>
> (Luke 10:41-42 NRSV)

The entire narrative drama of scripture can be presented with the simplest of props. A pitcher of water, a bowl, and a towel—simple staging that works for speaking about baptism, church membership, the miracle of the Exodus, and Jesus' command that we serve one another. Bread and wine are the only things needed to represent the grace of our Lord upon the cross. It doesn't take volumes to present our ethical principles; they are simply that we love one another and that we treat others as we would want them to treat us. The entire mission statement of the church can be found in the simple command Jesus gave—to go and make disciples of all nations. The entire organizational principle of the church can be found in the promise of our Lord to be present with us wherever two are three are gathered in his name. The genius of the small church is that it never travels very far from the simple things which are basic to the faith.

Simplicity means that the small church can function without a lot of sophistication. A certified accountant is not needed to count or distribute the small church's weekly offering. A paid staff person is not needed to run the children's program or schedule use of the church building. A single multi-purpose room with folding chairs can house the church and specialized altar ware and furniture may be counter productive.

Simplicity often spills over into the small church folk desiring a less complex message from the pulpit. If the message is clear and can be applied to daily life, it doesn't need a lot of literary allusions or historical footnotes. One small church attendee commented that preachers should wear their theological education like underwear, they should put it on but not let it show. As I will later argue, developing a culture of biblical literacy among the laity does more to insure theological consistency than elevating the educational requirements of the clergy.

Simple People

In another passage to the church at Corinth, Paul expressed this principle of simplicity saying:

> Consider your own call, brothers and sisters: not many of you were wise by human standards, not many were powerful, not many were of noble birth. But God chose what is foolish in the world to shame the wise; God chose what is weak in the world to shame the strong; God chose what is low and despised in the world, things that are not, to reduce to nothing things that are, so that no one might boast in the presence of God.
>
> 1 Corinthians 1:26-29

Paul here takes a sobering look at his small newly formed congregation in Corinth. He sees very few professionals and certainly no one who could be classified as wealthy. Christianity is not yet on the cultural radar, Paul has not been invited to the local ministerium or to join the Rotary, and the Saturday paper does not bother to list the church worship times. The church's only means of witness is through personal invitation; the society at large is oblivious to their presence. His observation is typical of many small churches today. Like the early Christians, many small churches notice that they tend to attract and assimilate more people from the lower economic strata. This is the small church's primary audience and their context for ministry. The few professionals that they have are long-time members who joined when the church was more prosperous.

Small churches have been more adversely affected than larger churches by the current cultural shift away from listening to religious institutions for values and direction. In the last fifty years the "First Church" congregations of American cities have gone from being cultural icons to being lesser players in the sport of public discourse. But small churches have gone from being minor league ball players to being locked out of the stadium and looking through a peep hole on the other side of the outfield fence. The news media and the "real" institutions of society, such as the public schools, local government, hospitals, and entertainment industry, consider the small church's communal witness to be mere street noise.

Paul had little reason to expect his little fledgling congregation to be noticed on the political stage, but he did not think that made them unimportant nor was Paul content to let them remain wallflowers at the social ball. Paul saw this current weak and small state in the context of God's propensity to use small things to bring about great change. He later shared with the Corinthians the personal vision God had given him:

> but [God] said to me, "My grace is sufficient for you, for power is made perfect in weakness." So, I will boast all the more gladly of my weaknesses, so that the power of Christ may dwell in me. Therefore I am content with weaknesses, insults, hardships, persecutions, and calamities for the sake of Christ; for whenever I am weak, then I am strong.
>
> 2 Corinthians 12:9-10

Paul, who is well educated, professionally trained, and born into a respected family, realizes that God stripped away all of this cultural baggage from him when he was converted to the Christian way. These things were for him rubbish that interfered with the work God had to do (Philippians 3:8). Perhaps the fact that God called such a common class of people to be the first converts in Corinth means that they started closer to the end product God had in mind. They enjoyed a natural humility and were not far from the kingdom of God.

Paul expresses a similar appreciation for the simplicity and genuine openness of spirit he first found among the Galatian people. He is markedly perplexed when they choose to run after the sophisticated rigmarole of a works-oriented religion. They had once received Paul because they saw in him a sincerity of heart and recognized truth. Now they were receiving orators and basing their acceptance upon the speaker's academic credentials. Once they centered their worship and fellowship life on Paul's message of forgiveness and grace. Why have they now substituted this simple dependence upon faith for an interest in liturgical etiquette and customs, which are alien to their native culture (Galatians 4:8-20)?

When small churches are healthy, they express their own sense of self identity as simple, humble folks without any tinge of self-pity. "Being simple is who we are," they say unashamedly. This doesn't mean that they are less intelligent, but rather that they have reached that place of wisdom where they can spot phony religious talk. When I was in seminary I served a small student church a hundred miles from school. Each weekend I would drive and rack my brain for ways to express what I was learning in seminary in a language that my congregation would understand. On the drive back to school, I felt humbled by the realization that they had taught me far more than I had taught them. Much of my classroom learning lacked authenticity and remained nebulous until they graciously mirrored back to me what I was trying to say. Some things were just not as important as I thought they were. Some things they already knew and had better ways of expressing. And in a few cases, what I learned in school turned out to be totally worthless in the context of a fellowship focused on the simplicity of faith.

Becoming a Clique

Simplicity in the small church, though, has to do with maintaining a homogeneous fellowship group. The intimacy that small church attendees value comes at the price of being inherently exclusive. Small congregations, in subtle and subconscious ways, maintain a welcoming posture towards those who are "like us," but often have little latitude with regard to those of a different class or culture. They may go out of their way to welcome an individual who shows up from a different race or economic strata than their own, but inviting that person into the intimate circle of the congregation's membership and fellowship life is a different matter. Birds of a feather flock together in small church life.

This, in itself, is not a particularly positive or Christ-like aspect of the congregation's behavior. It is to our collective shame, that as Martin Luther King put it, "eleven 'o clock on Sunday morning remains the most segregated hour of American weekly life."[2] This often observed effect is related to the small church's emphasis upon personal relationships and communal intimacy. Each member looks at the church fellowship as an extension of his or her own sense of identity. It becomes their extended family, their tribe. The congregation provides a middle way of comforting similarity for a person to retreat to in the midst of our sometimes confusingly diverse world.

Leaders, both lay and clergy, must realize and be soberly honest about this inherent defect in the small church as a fellowship organization. There are two fixes to this problem, both of which must be applied fervently and from the grassroots up. This problem that will not be corrected by applying a package program from the denominational officer by reciting a social creed. The people must wrestle with the issue of their own exclusive tendencies and see it as a defect in their Christian witness.

Going Beyond the Tribe

In general, the small church has inherited a tribal mindset, which tends to define the borders of who is in and who is out of the tribe because of physical appearance and location. Many of the people of a small country church worked in the small city fifteen miles away, but they never thought to invite someone who didn't live in their bedroom village to come to their church. The church's membership was entirely white, even though the village was gradually becoming more ethnically diverse. Further, the church leadership restricted some positions, including that of pastor, to men, because this tribe always had a "chief," never a "chieftess."

From Monday through Saturday, very few of these people are sexist, racist, or overly provincial in their attitudes. But how we define "tribe" depends upon context. When they attend a football game, these same people become fans who define their tribal boundary as all those who root for our team, no matter where they come from or what they look like. All around the world, the migration of individuals across borders and the globalization of our economy is forcing communal fellowships, whether they be business related, political, or religious, to become more inclusive in their definition of tribe.

Once again in writing to the small communal fellowships of Galatia, Paul points out how such a shift can occur in the church:

> There is neither Jew nor Greek, slave nor free, male nor female, for you are all one in Christ Jesus. If you belong to Christ, then you are Abraham's seed, and heirs according to the promise.
>
> (Galatians 3:28-29 NIV)

After pointing to various tribal boundaries, Paul states how the individual's relationship to Christ becomes the new boundary for the fellowship. It doesn't matter where one is located, or one's language, or who one's parents were, the church is defined simply as those who belong to Christ. Paul must have preached this radical concept fervently wherever he went, because he later manages the Herculean task of persuading the tradition-bound elders in Jerusalem to accept his diverse, formerly pagan, converts from Greece as full members of the faith. Then delivering the *grand reversal* that comes with God's reign to the traditional tribal boundaries, he invites the Corinthians to donate famine relief to their brothers and sisters in Jerusalem (Acts 11:28-30; 1 Corinthians 16:1-3).

While inclusiveness is a well accepted component of the small church member's understanding of Jesus' teachings, applying it to congregational behavior requires constant verbal reinforcement. In every aspect of our fellowship life, we must speak the truth that our fellowship is composed of all those who belong to Christ. It must be spoken specifically in the following contexts:

> Whenever the church nominates its church officers and leaders, it must intentionally think about who it considers for each post. Invite men to teach Sunday school as often as women. Invite women to serve as trustees as often as men. Address age discrimination constantly. Include youth in the decision-making process as trustees and board members. Keep seniors connected. The shift to evening meetings and email notification of the agenda often leaves those who can't drive at

night or access the internet feeling excluded. Assign someone to deliver the notes and offer to drive them to meetings, so that they can continue to participate.

Use inclusive language, not only from the pulpit, but in meetings, when referring to pastors and other church leaders.

Address the problems of racism, sexism, and ageism frequently from the pulpit and in small group studies. Many scriptures relate to these issues.

The real demographics of the neighborhood should be a frequent topic of conversation in the church. Leaders should guide people to see these statistics as an encouragement to reach out and to be invitational in specific ways.

Two things need to be said about this last point:

First, laity complain that their church cannot grow because the neighborhood is largely another religious group or attends some other dominant church of the region. When one church or faith group dominates a region, a large number of people have become disenfranchised by that church. Without being adversarial, many small churches have specifically made efforts to provide a church home for these disaffected people. Other churches in the neighborhood of a large fundamentalist church have tailored their advertisements to show that they are an accepting, non-judgmental congregation, inclusive of women in leadership. Positioning oneself in contrast to the predominant culture of a neighborhood is the proper appeal of the small membership church.

Second, the percentage of people who have a church home has dropped to about 40%. This means that six out of every ten houses surrounding the church have residents in need of a church home. Successful small churches count the open doors rather than the closed ones. The middle way of small church evangelism does not seek to convert those who have already have a religious practice which works for them, nor does it ignore its immediate neighborhood. It invites the people who live nearby, realizing that the church's presence may be the only witness to Christ these people encounter .

The small church building, whether located at a rural crossroad or in the midst of an urban neighborhood, reminds the community that Christ remains relevant even in our secular era. One elderly man who had become entirely deaf, and partially blind, was asked why he continued to make the effort to arrange transportation and attend a church service he could no longer hear or enjoy. He responded, "It is my witness. My presence tells people that the church still matters to me."

This simplicity of witness is what drives many small churches to pour so much effort into community vacation Bible school programs, even though their own membership is well beyond having small children. Small churches also host free clinics, twelve step programs, food banks, and after school mentoring programs, even though their members may have very little need of these services.

The corollary to this is that small churches violate the principle of simplicity when they abandon their neighborhood. In the changing neighborhoods of our country many small churches have not had a new member from their immediate neighborhood join for many years. The supporting membership has fled the city, but because they love their building, they continue to drive in from the suburbs to worship there. The neighborhood, instead of seeing these church buildings as witnesses to Christ, knows them to be symbols of institutional power or racism. Oblivious to this perception, these misplaced congregations are often perplexed when they become the target of vandalism.

Near to where I live a small church recently closed. The denominational executive, who was present at its last service, publicly commented that the church began to die forty years before when they had refused to receive an African-American family into membership. This distant act of racism was compounded by an ongoing refusal to look for ministries that would relate the congregation to its new neighbors. What is important to note is that as time goes by a congregation may become repentant about its attitude. But reconnecting with a shunned neighborhood is a task that becomes exponentially more difficult as time goes by. The vigilant and honest self-examination of one's neighborhood context may prevent a painful future closing.

Successful small churches are proactive about any changes in their community. Their leaders do their homework and consult with local realtors for clues in understanding demographics in the community. Each new resident has a different set of needs, which the wise church incorporates into its plans for programs and evangelism.

The membership of one church I served was largely upwardly mobile professional families, with a mix of retirees, some of whom still lived within walking distance of the church. The aging houses immediately near the church were gradually being broken into duplexes and apartments. Falling housing values made the few remaining single-family homes attractive as starter homes. The census data revealed that the average resident of our ZIP Code had lived there less than four years. Given the transient nature of this community, how should we have done evangelism?

We expected that most of the neighbors did not expect to be part of a long-term intimate church family relationship, nor could they be expected to stick around if they joined. Increasingly our active laity and church leaders came from further away. But the people of the neighborhood appreciated the after-school children's program, which cared for their young children. They also came out for the block party sponsored by the local clergy group. They also noticed when church members began to clean and repair the neighborhood park. For this church, doing local evangelism was not about finding new members; it was about serving the community.

Outside the Box

One way the small church can maintain its homogeneous simplicity is by entering into externally complex relationships. The people who actually join the small church may be all of a similar social class, ethnicity, and theological bent, but they can comfortably establish a sibling relationship with another small congregation that is different on any or all these grounds. Because small congregations have the security of knowing their own members well, they have the freedom to explore and the willingness to tolerate more diversity in their relationships with other organizations. The small congregations that I served were far more interested in my involvement in the local clergy group than the larger congregations have been. When small and large churches have been together in programmatic clusters or regional ministries, the lay participation and enthusiasm from the small the churches has been more consistent and visionary than that of the larger churches.

The people of one small Maine town thought nothing was unusual about their United Methodist Church sharing a vacation Bible school with the neighboring Roman Catholic congregation. The two small congregations quickly grasped the benefits of sharing resources and actually had fun working out how to tailor the curriculum so that it didn't step on anyone's theological toes.

Throughout this book we will return to the relationship that congregations share when they yoke, form a circuit, or establish a group ministry in order to fund pastoral compensation. Denomination executives who guide such marriages say that it is akin to herding cats. Each congregation knows that they need the shared relationship in order to pay the preacher, but they are suspicious, and often openly hostile, about the process. There are so many unknowns. If they form a circuit of three churches this year to afford a clergy, will they need four or five churches next year? *We don't know if we can change our worship time, and what about special services like Christmas Eve and Easter sunrise? Isn't the denomination just doing this because they eventually want to merge us? Which parsonage gets the pastor's family?*

Entering into shared ministry is a process. Certain steps need to follow in order and certain tasks cannot be left incomplete. Questions like those above need to be openly received and honestly answered, even if "we don't know." is the best current answer. A competent facilitator and active guide for the process is necessary. This consultant needs to meet with the rank and file of each congregation and spend the time to ensure that the people own the outcome. They may encounter open hostility towards the denomination for initiating the process. Another emotion to recognize is the grief tat congregations feel over their loss of independence. The stigma against multi-church circuits is part of the low sense of self esteem within many small churches.

Shared ministry between small congregations is the most exciting and fertile field for ministry within our country. In a larger parish or shared ministry, appropriately trained ordained pastors supervise a complex coalition of congregations working together. No other place offers the same potential for life-long career fulfillment in one location. It is also the one place where the full diversity of the spiritual gifts and skills of the laity can be fully realized. Those who have the gift to speak, speak, and those who have nurturing gifts find ways to act as shepherds. When it works well, there is a teamwork that puts clergy and laity, not only on the same page, but side by side in the trenches of sharing Christ with a world in need.

A shared ministry, however, will not work well if it is not established well. It cannot be entered into as a last minute effort to fund a particular salary or to place an unappointed clergy. The appropriate process is outlined in *Partnersteps* by Edward Kail and Julia Kuhn Wallace (published by Discipleship Resources). Note the following table of steps and missteps:

Step 1: Explore and come to consensus about the fundamental purpose of a church.	Misstep: Enter into a shared relationship merely for the sake of survival.
Step 2: Develop understandings about current identity. Who are we separately? What do we have in common?	Misstep: Failure to develop sufficient trust. People need to know that other churches share similar values and hopes.
Step 3: Establish a process for decision making that all can buy into.	Misstep: Perception that the results have been forced from outside the church.
Step 4: Plan for appropriate staffing.	Misstep: Hire the staff before doing steps one through three.
Step 5: Establish the appropriate structure for managing the shared ministry.	Misstep: Keep in place or adopt structures which don't fit the new reality.
Step 6: Evaluate and revisit the process.	Misstep: Fix in cement the structures and decisions established during implementation.

One concern denominational leadership often faces in entering into this process is the cost of appropriate leadership. As the process is implemented, the congregation may be reluctant to pay their share of an outside consultant's fee. If other denominational officials acquiesce and attempt to perform this function themselves, they are likely to fail. This happens, first, because they lack the time and patience to work the full process. Second, they are unprepared for the latent mistrust of the larger body, which is present in most small churches. What is important is not simply walking through the steps, but rather cultivating real ownership by the congregations for their emerging shared ministry. Both the congregations and the denominational leadership need to get out of the "problem solving mode," where the only concern they share is that of getting a pastor to agree to come. They need instead to work in a "transition mode," with its emphasis upon choosing a new future, perhaps even being served by an interim minister who has no stake in the outcome.

Though the denominational executive is usually the person who starts this process rolling, churches need to ask early who else to invite to the conversational table. A small congregation of another denomination or maybe a mission organization, such as an economic ministry, may seek to become a founding member of a new shared ministry. It is better to draw the initial circle too large and provide opportunity for groups to opt out than to start too small and scramble to bring additions into the already started process.

Shared ministries unite diverse congregations in a united witness to their community. Congregations who work together are more apt to have a stated set of goals and positive vision for the future. Having sister congregations creates an atmosphere of mutual accountability. Church leaders become energized when they realize that the shared ministry is capable of doing things on a local level according to a plan that they formulated themselves.

Simplicity Means Playing the Hand You Are Dealt

I am a poor bridge player. I tend to bid and play my cards based upon the strength of a few flashy high cards. If I have an ace in a suit, that's the one I want to bid. A few royalty in one color and I'm off. But those who play bridge well do two things. First, they constantly count all the cards on the table, noticing what has been played and who is likely to play a trump on an ace. They play their middle value cards well. It's not the person who gets the easy tricks who wins, but the one who consistently play jacks on tens and nines on eights.

A small congregation is highly unlikely to have a powerhouse hand with royalty in every suit. They may have one thing they do reasonably well, and few supporting qualities. They may have a nice choir or a lively ministry to the seniors of the community. It is important that they don't overplay their hand by trying to be good at everything. It is in the nature of a small church that there will be areas of what is otherwise considered normal church life in which they will be lacking. They may have a void in youth ministry or have just a few children in Sunday School. Every small church is dealt a hand that lacks something. The important thing is not to obsess over what is lacking, but rather to play the hand you are dealt the best possible way.

To take this analogy further, the small church needs to be aware of its strong suit. This is where counting the cards and knowing what is in everyone else' hand is important. Churches should not think of themselves as in competition with the other churches of the neighborhood. Rather, one has to know what needs are being met by the other social and religious institutions of the region in order to play your own suit well. If you look in your hand and discover a weak area, it is likely that someone else is strong in that same suit. Why not cooperate with that other congregation? No matter how small a congregation, there will be some ministry that it does well. Churches, like people, have their calling. It is important that they take pride and shape their identity around the ministries that bring their people enjoyment.

Newcomers tend to arrive in a congregation with certain preconceived ideas. I tend to enjoy playing clubs in bridge, but that prejudice only serves me well about one quarter of the time. Many new pastors arrive in a church looking to play their favorite suit. Pastors may envision a strong music ministry centered on the frequent use of fresh contemporary choruses. They may even bring an ace to the table in the form of their own musical gifts. But what if this vision is an ace without any of the congregation's cards to support it?

In my region, newly ordained pastors are given two contradictory pieces of advice. Some people say to them, "Don't attempt to change anything for at least eighteen months. You have to give people a chance to know and trust you." Others say, "Your first year is your honeymoon. Any changes you want to make, do it then." Both forms of advice are worthless! Every pastor is duty bound to listen and explore their congregation's strengths and weaknesses. Pastors are not assigned to a church to play their own hand. Often a sensitive listener will discover that the congregation has become sidetracked away from their own purpose and mission. The lay leadership may be burned out. They may have taken on projects for which they are neither gifted nor comfortable. If this is the case, make changes by giving people permission to abandon unsuitable dreams. The small church has a limited hand of cards.

Another question begs an answer: Who determines what a church's strong suit is? God does! The pastor's role is to be a team leader who supports the congregation in doing its ministry. Whatever role a pastor plays as a change agent, pastors of small church must help these churches rediscover the simplicity of playing their own best suit.

A peaceful joy comes into the life of a congregation when it is given the permission, in the words of Henry David Thoreau, to simplify, simplify, simplify!

1 *Walden* by Henry David Thoreau (State Street Press, 2000) p.106.

2 Martin Luther King, Jr., *"Remaining Awake through a Great Revolution,"* sermon preached at the National Cathedral in Washington, D.C., March 31, 1968.

CHAPTER THREE

WHAT MAKES THE SMALL CHURCH SMALL?

What then is a small church? Some people answer this question with a number. Some experts identify a small church as one in which the worshiping congregation has fewer than seventy-five people. Other writers place this number at a hundred worshipers, or at 125, or even as high as 200. By any of these figures, the small church remains the most common form of religious organization in America.

While the average congregation gathers fewer than 100 people for worship each week, the average church attendee participates in a large church. If this math feels fuzzy, imagine five one-gallon buckets with two trout swimming in each one. Now imagine two five-gallon buckets with six trout each, and one twenty-gallon bucket with twenty-five fish. The average size bucket would be one-gallon, but the average number of trout would be in the largest bucket. You would have to ask the trout to find out which bucket was the best. When Jesus calls us to be fishers of people, he doesn't tell us which size bucket to bring.

In the United Methodist Church, 3,000 congregations have fewer than 25 members on their rolls. These micro-sized churches have another twenty to thirty constituents–people who consider themselves part of the church even though they haven't joined. The total nurturing footprint of the smallest churches of this denomination numbers around 150,000 people, or about the population of a city such as Tallahassee, Florida or Springfield, Massachusetts.[1] Meanwhile, the largest 3,000 churches of the denomination have over 3.5 million members on their roles, and they are growing at a surprising rate. Even with fewer constituents, you can picture these large churches of the United Methodist denomination, that is those with an attendance over 1,500 a week, providing nurture to all those who call the metro area of New York their home. According to the U.S. Census 2000 data, New York City's population is 8,008,278.

The situation is analogous to looking at the lakes and streams that dot our land. While most streams and bodies of water are small, the few great lakes and larger rivers hold most of the country's free standing water. It would be silly for an ecologist to speak about how large bodies of water are in some way "more efficient" than ponds and streams. While small streams are extremely vulnerable to environmental changes, it would be unusual for an expert to pronounce that larger rivers are inherently healthier. Nor has anyone proposed consolidating ponds into lakes as a way to improve our ecosystem.

Health and Size

Why is merger such a popular proposal for making small churches healthier? The driving force for church consolidation is an ignorance about God's plan for the scalability of the church. Those who worship in larger churches often lack an intuitive appreciation of the smaller congregation's role in fulfilling Jesus' great commission. The mechanisms that cause a small church to stall and fail to carry out its mission are not related to its size, but rather to lack of health.

Healthy congregations make disciples and often grow numerically up to the top boundary of their intended size. For them, the work of making disciples spills out beyond their walls and becomes hard to quantify in statistics like average worship attendance or number on the membership role. The vitality of many small churches shines when you consider their nurturing footprint (members plus friends and non-attending families who look to the church for pastoral care) and their community outreach or mission giving. Even healthy churches sometimes face difficulties in finding appropriate pastoral leadership, but when they face those periods, they have a sufficient understanding of what it means to be a church that they survive. Many small churches witness to their vitality by continuing to make disciples and have inspiring worship even though their pulpit is filled by a supply preacher for months or years.

Unhealthy churches fail to make disciples and fail to be disciples of Jesus. They shrink to the minimum number of attendees needed to keep their doors open. They perform by rote ritual the worship and programs expected of them and only grudgingly participate in activities and offerings that go beyond their walls. They are theologically myopic, attending only to those scriptures and aspects of the faith that reinforce their institutional behavior. Inwardly focused, they see only the needs of the church, not the needs of the people outside the church. Unhealthy churches can be large or small, but if they do not reverse their disease, they will decline until they disappear.

These churches are usually marked by a fixation on what the pastor is doing or not doing. A wide gulf exists between the jobs the people expect their clergy to do and the tasks they leave for themselves as laity to do. If someone suggests shifting a task, such as visiting the shut-ins from the clergy side of the register to a shared ministry with lay people, an uproar happens. An even greater outcry may occur when the pastor express an interest in something that has been considered off limits to clergy, such as an audit of individual giving records. A further indicator of this situation is how often members will complain, saying how the expense of keeping a minister is killing the church. The comment will be made, even if they like their current pastor and even if the pastor is present and likely to take the comments personally. In general there is a failure to see the minister as a person with a similar Christian call and the same humanity as the "normal" people of the church.

When churches lack vitality, they enter a pastor-consuming cycle. Whether through petty conflicts, apathy, or a combination of the two, they diminish the enthusiasm of any pastor. This cycle is like an eating disorder, a systemic anorexia. The congregation, no matter what its initial size, has fixed its behavior, which is self-destructive and will cause it to die. Meanwhile the pillars of the church will keep an unrealistic image of the church. They will see themselves as fat with ministry and potential, when in reality they are gauntly malnourished by their own selfishness. Gone are the days when a pastor feels welcomed to make a career of serving this congregation. The leaders of Old First Church may fondly remember the twenty-year, or more, tenure of the beloved senior pastor who served during the church's golden era, but now they are caught in an every other year pastoral change, a cycle which marks a deeply troubled congregation.

Declining churches, no matter what their initial size, tend to attract the kind of clergy who make promises, but then fail to meet expectations. After all, for the declining church, the expectation for each new pastor is to do all the things that the former pastor did, but without the staff and the resources cut from the budget in order to pay the pastoral salary. These "set-up-to-fail" clergy display co-dependent personality traits; that is, they have a lowered sense of self esteem, which causes them to over-commit to their work. They may be unaware of how driven their behavior is by this inner need to win approval. They do not want to be like the last two or three pastors who failed to meet the congregation's expectations. They listen to the laundry list of complaints people are voicing about the previous pastors, and then set out to do the impossible. And when the impossible cannot be done, they fall back on plan B, which is to make themselves indispensable.

This "co-dependence," where the church needs the pastor and the pastor neurotically needs the church to need him or her is achieved by hijacking some vital area of church life. They may lock the laity out of participation in the worship service, or take control of the finances, or put the church office in such a state of chaos that they alone know where the membership rolls are kept or how to put out the newsletter. Initially the people rejoice that the new pastor is "taking charge," but soon this unhealthy violation of the natural church process leads to conflict. The congregation and pastor lose sight of what it means to work together as a team. In a healthy church, the relationship between clergy and key lay leadership sets a tone of trust and mutual respect that serves as an example to all the other committees of the church. When a dependency relationship has been fostered, both by the unreasonable expectations voiced by laity and by irrational co-dependent self-expectations acted upon by the clergy, the entire decision-making process becomes strained. Each party stakes out his or her own territory and defends it against incursions by the other. The pastor cannot sustain his or her heroic effort to run it all and begins to resent the laity, complaining that they lack the commitment or skills to support the church. The laity very quickly pick up on this change in attitude. They hear the pastor talking about "your church," where the pastor once said, "Our church." Even before the pastor has started looking to move, the lay people are rightfully concerned that this attitude is dangerous to their survival as a congregation. In the small church, survival is the primary concern, and the lay leadership will "cut their losses" and seek to get rid of a pastor, even one they like, to avoid the suggestion that they lack the commitment or the resources to continue to be a church. For many small churches, conflict and rapid clergy turnover feels safer than working through an extended process of redefining lay-clergy roles. For many small-church pastors, moving every two years feels safer than dealing with the issues generated by their personal style of leadership.

Other small churches have conceded themselves into the opposite situation; they have an ineffective pastor who has served them for many years. Here again, early on in the clergy-laity relationship, a co-dependent situation became the norm. The pastor marked a certain turf as his or her own and communicated that message. Healthy, long-term pastorates have a dynamic division of lay-clergy roles, where the functions each performs gets redefined constantly throughout the relationship. When churches lack vitality, no matter their size, a false equilibrium becomes established. The laity accept a false notion that they are deficient and dependent upon the pastor that they have. They may accept a pastor who fails to communicate spiritual passion, or who may be controlling, or even an abusive personality, because they have been made to feel that they are lucky to have this person who does the one thing they cannot do themselves. For many small churches, this association of their survival with one particular clergy is reinforced by denominational executives who tell them that they are lucky to have a pastor who will serve so few people. Meanwhile, many clergy remain in situations that are no longer challenging or providing any opportunities for real ministry because their sense of self-esteem has become dependent upon being the only hope for this small church to survive.

For both the church that has co-dependently clung to de-energizing clergy and the church that sees a constant parade of short-term pastorates an intervention needs to occur to put the clergy-lay relationship back in balance. Here is where the placement of a trained interim minister or the use of a transitional process is important. To expect a new pastor to fix all the problems, serve as the church's pastor forever, and re-establish a healthy and flexible teamwork between clergy and laity is extremely difficult. The church needs an outside consultant, who does not have a long-term stake in the situation, to guide the congregation and clergy in an honest appraisal and expression of need.. Unfortunately, the co-dependent cycle, unless broken, will provide failing churches of every size with clergy who are disinclined to reconnect the laity to their shared task of making disciples. A church that does not effectively invite people into discipleship lacks vitality, and acquires a poor reputation. This cycle goes on until a church becomes "small," and then they simply accept pulpit supply.

When churches are healthy, they encourage each Christian to participate to the fullest extent of his or her talents, resources, and gifts. Even a church with twenty-five in attendance includes several people who enjoy reading scripture and sharing the liturgical roles of worship leadership. One of these lay liturgists might even preach quite well, when asked to substitute. With two or three churches of this size, the supervising clergy will work with a small cadre of people, who, with sufficient training, can be very edifying when they preach and lead adult classes. Healthy small churches soon find themselves with an oversupply of those who use their gifts to share the gospel. Far from taking what they can get, they give and give, often supplying services at local nursing homes and at neighboring churches who need pulpit supply.

When a church is small, it is a mistake to think that the difficulty providing appropriate clergy is simply a problem related to their size. Because denominational leaders focus on the problem of providing clergy to every situation, they usually fall into the trap of assuming that small churches are inefficient and unsustainable. This failure to grasp the small church paradigm of scalability hampers ministry.

Over the last few decades the majority of new Christians, as well as new church attendees, look first to larger churches for their church home. The trend is basic: the larger a church is, the more likely it will grow. We cannot assume that this trend is irreversible. Nor can we assume that small churches have failed in reaching the current generation. I believe that this trend is a positive thing in that it forces small churches to be more intentional about their mission. They need to identify how they are fulfilling the great commission and how their particular local outreach positively attracts others to Christ. No longer can a church, especially a small church, think of itself as a chapel serving the needs of its members. Small church values may not be popular with the mainstream of our culture, but they still need to be stated and lived out in parallel to the witness of the more progressive, seeker-friendly churches.

Other Definitions

Another way to define the small church is to say that it includes less than a few dozen families, or 200 members reported on the church rolls. Denominations differ in how they count families and receive members. These numbers offer little clarity. Small rural churches often have their own independent way of viewing who is and isn't a part of their church. One attendee of such a church considered every family in the community, with the exception of a few Roman Catholics, as members because her preacher did all the marriages and burials in the region. Another, when asked how many families there were in the church said, "One; we're all related here."

The small church is better defined in terms of its social structure. We are greatly indebted to authors, such as Carl Dudley, who define the small church as a single cell organism in *Making the Small Church Effective*. The small church is like a single-celled organism or a self-contained village with a wall around it. The activities are planned so that everyone can participate together rather than having separate age or interest groups. Decisions are made at meetings that are open for everyone to attend. Separate committee meetings are rarely called. When a church ceases to be a small church, this structure that says, "We do all things together," gives way to a structure that now says, "We each participate in our own way." Diversity of programs and activities is the hallmark of medium and larger churches.

The defining mark of the small church is simplicity. When thirty or even fifty people meet together each week for worship, they soon know each other well enough not to need separate small groups to build the sense of intimacy, which is an essential part of the Christian experience. The development of Christian believers into effective disciples seems to require small-group experience. When a church's weekly attendance passes seventy-five, more complex and programmatic solutions seem necessary to incorporate every potential disciple for Christ into a small group. The church's worship experience itself ceases to function as a small group in the minds of the relatively new Christian.

It is hard to pin down this boundary between the small church and the medium-sized church in terms of numbers because we are dealing with how the experience of faith is perceived by the church attendee. Some churches of seventy-five feel like medium-sized churches and actively encourage each attendee to participate in the Sunday School class or fellowship group that meets their individual needs. Other churches whose attendance reaches 100 may have such a small fellowship feel about them that they do well to encourage everyone to attend everything which they offer in terms of programs.

However subjective this boundary between a small and medium-sized congregation is, some very real social barriers make it important to distinguish between these two types of churches. A church growing from small to medium-sized will encounter a high level of stress as it approaches this boundary. Long-time members will complain that things don't feel right, even though they may be enthusiastic about the church's growth. Subconsciously the congregation may sabotage their potential for growth and rebound repeatedly back to a smaller size. This oscillation between being the old familiar small church and being a "real church" with its own pastor is a common phenomena.

A medium-sized church can decline and the experience of worship feels like a small group. Not willing to admit that they have passed a boundary, the congregation and pastor continue to try to drum up enthusiasm for the things that were important when they were larger. Telling the declining congregation to invest in small groups or add more Sunday School classes is like telling a fish to drink more water. The worship experience each person is encountering on Sunday morning feels like a small group. Why not reorganize the church to find contentment in its current smaller size?

Churches need to have worship, administrative structures, and fellowship activities appropriate to their size. For a small church to grow and be vital before it reaches the small/medium boundary, the people must simply do what they already know to be the right thing in a more consistent way. To grow past the small-medium boundary line, for a small church to become a medium-sized church, requires abandoning the familiar. Here, the successful programs for growth require a counterintuitive leap of faith. The congregation often feels in turmoil because the leadership changes the form or number of worship services, adds committees, and develops new fellowship groups while perhaps abandoning the old faithful ones. The people will incarnate Jesus' words:

> No one sews a patch of un-shrunk cloth on an old garment, for the patch will pull away from the garment, making the tear worse. Neither do men pour new wine into old wineskins. If they do, the skins will burst, the wine will run out and the wineskins will be ruined. No, they pour new wine into new wineskins, and both are preserved.
>
> (Matthew 9:16-17 NIV)

In a similar way, a formerly medium-sized congregation requires a radical rethinking of its identity to find vitality and contentment after it has declined below about one hundred in worship. Often outside factors or a series of unintentional events are responsible for the decline. I know of a small city that from one census to the next lost half its population. In the decade that followed, all three of the formerly medium-sized United Methodist churches, one of the two Lutheran congregations, and the one medium-sized Presbyterian church dropped below 100 in worship and became small churches. Each experienced an extended period of chaotic discontent. Congregants said, "Well, we'll do better once we get a new pastor." People looked for an outsider to *save* the situation, failing to recognize that the environment itself was now very different.

A church consists of a group of people in a variety of complex relationships with each other. Radical shifts occur in those relationships at the small/medium church border. At the border congregational life no longer feels right, and the members will seek simple cause-and-effect answers rather than systemic answers to this perceived problem. People prefer to point to a tangible thing, like changing the hymnal or the time of worship, as the cause of the congregational unrest. Spiritual maturity calls us to step back from the situation and realize that since we have fewer people in attendance than we did a few years ago, the relationships we have will become less formal and more intimate. The role that various committees and officers play in the church will also change significantly. Some functions will now be handled by an individual relating directly to the pastor rather than by a committee relating to each other and the church board. In a later chapter we will look at how the pastor-laity relationship is markedly different between medium and small churches.

In many churches, this tendency to look for simple cause-and-effect answers to vent the perceived tension at the small/medium-sized church boundary leads to open conflict. This is true for both growing and declining situations and may simply be a necessary step for any organization bridging a social boundary. Having a church fight gives people an explanation for why they feel bad, even if it is the wrong explanation. (In *The Church Transition Workbook*, published by Discipleship Resources, I provide a process for moving through a time of change as well as a more thorough examination of the range of church sizes.)

Adding People

Another identifying mark of the small church concerns the way it assimilates members. A new person may show up one Sunday and they are recognized and greeted by name for several weeks. Then a storm happens and church is canceled for that week. The phone chain alerts everyone of this change–except the new attendee. Or the church may have an annual event, "the big box-lunch social," which is clearly shown in the bulletin, but what exactly it is, who is to come, what to bring, and even when the event takes place, is never explained. Each week the people of the church are friendly to the newcomer, but they never get beyond a few conversational pleasantries. No one is surprised when the new people stop coming. With a shrug, the church members say, "I bet they are now going to a larger church."

Every small church is like a medieval village, with a wall and sometimes a moat surrounding it. We may think that we are friendly: we've left the drawbridge down and the door isn't locked, but little effort is made to enable a visitor to take up residence. The small congregation's walls serve to protect the intimacy and simplicity of relationships within the church.

Visitors may feel pleasantly surprised by the inspiring simplicity of the worship. They look around and say to themselves, "It won't be hard for me to fit in with this group." With high expectations of being accepted and treated as one of the group, they are surprised by incidents in which they feel second-class, primarily because they have not lived there all their lives. The regulars do not explain local customs, rituals, or dialect. They are not told, for example, that they need to bring their own flatware to the potluck supper, or even what a "potluck" means. Missed communications abound.

The medium-sized church assimilates new members by having a program or small group designed especially for them. They have thought about how they look to outsiders and have in place mechanisms for identifying and informing newcomers of their traditions and entry points. The pastor plays a pivotal role in this process, often following up to ensure good communication. The small church, however, cannot improve its assimilation of new members by asking the pastor to do it. This expectation that visitors or outsiders have concerning assimilation within the church relates to the intimacy visitors see expressed among the church members. The pastor's glad handing feels phony compared to the real thing the small congregation has to offer.

To do well at assimilation, the small church needs to develop two qualities. First, a sense of identity, which is based upon our relationship with Christ, needs clear expression, woven into the fabric of the church's life. We may think that we belong to a small group, like a church, because we have years of shared relationships. We cannot simply hand over to a visitor the experiences of growing up together. We can honestly share with others the relationship and love we have in Christ. The small church members need to remind themselves constantly that they belong to each other not because of their shared history, but because of their shared faith in Jesus. The second need is a healthy dose of self-appreciation. Another way to describe this is to encourage a sober reflection that leads to understanding that small church life is a gift for sharing.

Individual church members will feel comfortable being outwardly friendly to the extent their own personality allows them. If they are shy people, no church growth program or prodding from the pastor will make them greet people more positively. If the church understands that, in Christ, everyone who walks through the door is a brother or sister, then the church will seek to meet the needs for fellowship that person has. Further, if the people of a congregation feel good about their church's work of making disciples, then the church will create additional bridges and openings across the social barrier that surrounds such an intimate fellowship as the small church.

The Microchurch

It may help to extend this concept of how single-cell, simple, small churches differ from multi-celled, more complex, medium-sized churches by examining the sub-group of small churches with less than thirty-five in attendance. Many of these churches function comfortably out of one- or two-room buildings. The size of the church facility and the size of the church budget are not too different from the square footage of a member's home or a family's budget. Maintaining the church is similar to maintaining one's personal home, and often one of the church families takes that task as a project. A neighbor may mow the grass and shovel snow from the sidewalk. Another member may show up with cleaning products from home. Because the microchurch is so small, it blurs the distinction between church and home.

This makes the microchurch highly economical and relatively resistant to the traumatic events that may cause neighboring small churches to close. The local economy may falter, but the microchurch with its faithful retiree membership base plugs along. The microchurch may tolerate an ineffective or abusive pastor in the same way that families often adapt to a disruptive member in their home. The programs offered by a nearby megachurch may influence people to leave other small churches, but for the long term members of the microchurch, leaving this place would be similar to abandoning one's home. When it comes to survivability, the microchurch fares better than other small churches, just as small churches often do better than their medium-sized sisters and brothers in handling external threats.

The very real dangers that these microchurches face stem from the congregation's inability to distinguish church and home. The church can become a chapel that serves only the needs of particular family and their friends. It can fail to invite those outside the family or fail to witness to the power of the Christian gospel. When a congregation moves into chapel mode, expectations of fulfilling Jesus' command to make disciples fall off of the collective radar screen. Visiting some microchurches today reminds one of how wealthy Victorian families would hire a minister to conduct services in one of the rooms of their mansions. Far from being vessels bringing the revolutionary and saving power of Christ's gospel to the meek of the earth, these chapels upheld the aristocratic status quo and put a religious stamp of approval on class segregation. In the same way, microchurches today may be co-opted to meet the psychological needs of the family who "owns the church." Often the controlling heads of these family chapels keep the church in existence, not because it serves the community, but because they feel too uncomfortable to join in fellowship with Christian meeting elsewhere.

These harsh words need to be heard to distinguish the healthy and vital microchurch from the unhealthy one. Chapel-mode congregations are inwardly focused. They generally have a presiding matriarch or patriarch who dominates the decision-making process. The energy of the congregation is focused on avoiding change, maintaining the status quo, and keeping the dominant family's leader happy. Pastors who serve these churches soon realize that their ministry falls within the expectations of head family. Even if they serve this little chapel all of their careers, they will remain outsiders. Their status resembles the hired gunfighter in the American West, paid to bring the message and little more.

A healthy microchurch may have a dominant family or individual, but these leaders will focus on external matters. Their pride and sense of ownership of the church relates to its role in the community. The congregation's energy focuses on improving their shared witness. Because they are led by laity who are not interested in having the church remain a particular way, healthy microchurches can do daring things. Some have turned over their facility to an outreach, such as a homeless shelter or a feeding program, while reserving only Sunday morning for their congregational use. Others have taken an active interest in meeting the needs of the children in a neighboring trailer park or high-rise. Still others serve as the senior center for the community. Because microchurches have little to lose and a simplicity of spirit, they can develop outreach programs that fit closely to the context of their community.

Grouped by Expectation

Perhaps a more useful way of grouping small churches concerns how the church's history and expectations relate to its current size. Using this distinction, small churches fall into three divergent groups.

Once Upon a Time

First, some churches shrunk in size. I describe these as "once upon a time" churches. When a church declines past the boundary between the medium and small sized congregation, a system-wide reorganization becomes necessary. Not only must the church find a new way to fill the pulpit, it needs to adapt its facility and program to the needs of a smaller congregation.

You know that you are in a "once upon a time" church when:

– The choir outnumbers the congregation.

– Committees listed in the annual report never meet.

– The list of previous pastors reveals a "golden era" when pastors all stayed more than ten years, followed by decade when pastors stayed about five years, followed by a decade when pastors are shared with another church, are semi-retired, or are bi-vocational.

– The building contains rooms that are not used.

– The fellowship hall has a stage, but no one remembers the last play. This space is now a junk catch-all.

– Octogenarians in worship outnumber the children in the nursery.

The church I attended while in college is typical of a "once upon a time" church. When I went there, the church struggled to find space for both the children and adults who participated in the Sunday morning church school. Some who attended were students at the neighboring college and we were not surprised to see one of our college professors teaching Sunday School or washing the dishes after a potluck. Over the years the church has been proud of the half-dozen young people it sent into the ministry and the money it raised for foreign missions.

Today, however, this church has very few young people and rarely has a visitor from the college. The past decades have brought a variety of pastors to the congregation, none staying much more than five years. The population of the town has dropped in half, and the working middle class is nearly extinct. The average worship attendance is now 61, about one-third of its size four decades earlier. In the meantime, the college has nearly doubled in size and even though the church remains only a block from the campus, there are very few contacts between the two communities. The students who do attend church prefer to drive into the contemporary services offered at other churches in town. The professors, who tend today to be untenured and transient, also choose to attend the larger churches. The pastor now shared with four other churches has little time for campus ministry.

Is this a case of mid-sized church experiencing a temporary loss of congregants? Or is it a small church, facing the same barriers to growth that were spoken of earlier in this chapter? For this and other "once upon a time" churches, the path to congregational health may not lead them back to their glory days. This congregation, like many others, needs a middle way. If they become stagnant and discouraged because they are unable to do what they once did, there will be no way to stop the declining attendance and they will eventually close. The "once upon a time" church does not need to grow back to its old size, but it does need to engage in a form of disciple-making that reflects its current size. The church may not be able to provide the kind of campus ministry that draws students to worship services, but the people can participate with other community churches in sponsoring events that minister to the students and college staff. One small example is baking cookies for student orientation and extending personal invitations for home-cooked meals to the students who remain on campus over Thanksgiving break.

The transition from mid-sized to small church is a drastic change, even when it occurs gradually. The church leadership needs to manage this transition by fostering open conversations about the church's new identity. The congregation that clings to its old identity is reminiscent of the Hollywood film star who, having lost youthful looks, refuses to transition into more mature roles. Many "once upon a time" churches live an unhappy existence of clinging to their former glory. When a traumatic event, such as clergy misconduct or a dramatic population shift, caused this decline, this incident in the congregation's history needs to be named and grieved. Often these congregations seldom have emotional energy to spare for rehashing the past. Discovering what God is calling the church to be today remains the primary task for lay and clergy leadership of these situations. No matter their former size, they must fashion a new identity consistent with an acceptance of their new status as a small church. Often this new self-understanding leads to radical changes in building use, committee structure, programming, and expectations for pastoral leadership.

Up and Coming

The second category is "up and coming" churches. These churches are either new church starts or churches clearly identified as having a potential to become significantly larger. They are temporarily small and are marked by an expectation among in the pew that the church will double in size quickly and often. Unfortunately, many "church growth programs" and the approach of some clergy and denominational officials to all the small churches under their care attempts to transplant this attitude into the hearts of people attending churches which have little chance of being "up and coming" churches. Attitudes, like orchids, cannot simply be transplanted to soil that is not appropriate to them. You cannot will a church into growth by telling them that they should become just like the "up and coming" church down the street.

An example of an "up and coming" small church is Faith UMC, a church that I currently serve as pastor. The congregation was organized in the late 1800s in the farmland northwest of Pittsburgh. By the end of the 1950s the community around the church became one of the choice neighborhoods of the city. With the encouragement of the denomination, the congregation built a modern church facility on a larger adjacent property. Suburban growth brought the potential for rapid church growth, but this congregation failed to grow. The new church building remained relatively small, and the church failed to compete with the programs offered by neighboring larger churches or the prestige of wealthier congregations.

In 1994, the church no longer seemed viable and plans were made to sell the facility. The part-time pastor sent to close the facility, Rev. Larry Fink, saw instead a glimmer of hope. He did close the church, but before selling the property, he offered to the faithful few members a chance to meet together as a study group and prayerfully explore what God willed in these circumstances. With his leadership that small group rediscovered what it meant to be a church and embraced a personal commitment to the process of making disciples. In a few weeks this group had formulated a plan for becoming a vital congregation, and they re-opened with a new name and a mission to be a more inclusive and inviting congregation. For the next ten years, until his death, the Rev. Fink taught this congregation to be open to change and to the leading of the Holy Spirit. The church sold its pews, turned its sanctuary into a multi-use space, and converted the old parsonage into a preschool. It produced a yearly pageant, called the Medieval Feast, to raise money for missions. The people focused outwardly, seeking a multitude of ways to volunteer in the life of their community.

When the weekly worship attendance grew to about fifty, the congregation began to think about what they should do to keep the church growing. They could consolidate their gains and settle into to being a happy little congregation living snugly within the limits of their building, which was designed to seat about 100 people. They instead made a bold decision to keep growing despite the cost. Just seven years after they closed one church, this congregation boldly took on a 1.4 million-dollar building project. The architecture of the new sanctuary is innovative, flexible, and inviting. Large, plate glass windows encourage the people to look out into their community while they worship. Movable seats and a movable altar denote a spirit that refuses to be contained in a traditional structure.

Faith UMC remains a statistically small church with less than 150 members. Its programs and attitude move it into the next size range. The administrative structure already includes fully functioning committees where other churches this size would have only work area leaders or would handle these functions in a monthly council meeting. A culture of expectation has been nurtured in the congregation, so that they anticipate and put in to place practices and structures to accommodate future growth.

Growing small churches inevitably face the issue of whether or not they should divide the congregation by offering multiple worship services. When Faith UMC began its building project, part of its existing sanctuary and some of its parking area could no longer be used due to the construction. This change was anticipated, and the church immediately offered another worship service to prevent overcrowding. Two years later, when they moved into their larger sanctuary, discussion focused on whether to drop this new service since they now had plenty of room. The people learned that many of the new attendees at Faith UMC came into the church through the early service. One of the attractions to new members was the fact that the church gave people a choice as to when to attend worship. The lessons from that multiple worship experience are important to growing churches, not because they keep the members comfortable in a small building longer, but because they open the door for new people to discover the church. This does not mean that adding a second worship service will cause a church to grow, but having multiple services is an important component of the transition from small to mid-sized. In every small congregation a vocal number of people will complain, with good reason, that splitting the worshiping congregation makes having the intimate fellowship in this church harder to maintain. The successful "up and coming" church listens carefully to the concern expressed and then works hard to build loving relationships while adding the additional worship services it needs to grow.

Bob Whitesel, in his book *Growth by Accident, Death by Planning: How Not to Kill a Growing Congregation*, confirms that returning to a single worship service often halts a church's growth, causing the church to plateau at a size smaller than what their building can accommodate. He also cautions that new church starts as well as small churches who are growing need to be careful about shifting away from the values that started the church's growth. Some growing churches shift away from the intensity of prayer for the un-churched outside community, praying instead only for their own people when they become established mid-sized congregations. Others become clergy oriented, hiring professional staff instead of doing the work of lay empowerment. Still other "up and coming" churches fall into the trap of taking unwarranted financial risks. The fiscally conservative mind-set that marks the small church is often jettisoned when rapid growth happens, only to leave the congregation stuck when income projections don't pan out.

Pastors serving "up and coming" churches often feel like they are straddling an ice flow, with one foot on one ice chunk and the other on a separate piece that is drifting away. The support for what they are currently doing is related to the past. Acting in anticipation and planning for what needs to be, requires them to have one foot in the future. In some areas, such as budgeting, the church leadership needs to be conservative. In other areas, such as in starting a new worship service, the church leadership needs to do their homework, see what factors maintain growth in similar situations, then take a bold leap into the future.

Always Small

This category may include the majority of the small churches. These congregations have always been small membership churches. These "always small" churches display, in their architecture, organizational structure, and programs, a contented sense of being the right size for what they have been called to do. Being small fits them like the right cut of a suit fits the person. They are what I call the real churches of "the middle way" because for them vitality depends upon finding their way between the unreasonable expectations of those who think they should grow and the stagnation that will occur if they don't constantly look for ways to change and become more vital.

The five churches that make up the Glasgow Larger Parish are typical of this category. Each of these congregations began in the late 1800s, serving the rural ridge on the eastern flank of the Allegheny Mountains. The ups and downs of the coal mining industry has left this Appalachian region pocketed with small crossroads towns stripped of economic hopes. Each of the church buildings, which were constructed at the beginning of the 20th century, accommodate about a hundred in the sanctuary, and about half that in fellowship and educational spaces. The churches ebb and flow in membership, taking turns from time to time as to which point of the charge is growing and which is "backsliding." Totaled together, they consistently have enough members and financial resources to maintain the one full-time pastor and one part-time pastor who serve them.

Consider these observations:

– This rural region, which consists of over 100 square miles, contains no growing mainline churches. While some people do drive off of the ridge to the large churches of the city, the majority of the residents look to a small church pastor for their spiritual needs.

– The economic depression of the community, the history of clergy movement (changing every three to four years), and the long stability of their current size combine to make these congregations reluctant to make a major change for the sake of growth. What incentive do they have, given their 125-year history of doing church the current way, to give up their buildings and to relocate as a merged congregation?

– These congregations have developed a culture that promotes lay empowerment. Day-to-day problems tend not to be solved by the pastors, but by local leadership. The churches send more than their share of people to the district lay academy and have a number of people trained as lay speakers. Parish Bible studies are well attended, and having a mature faith is considered to be a prerequisite for church office. Biblical literacy is high, and there is an expectation that everyone be capable of sharing their faith.

– Instead of being internally focused and falling into the trap of becoming little family chapels, these congregations enthusiastically support functions held by the larger parish. The churches see the whole rural ridge as their parish. When prayer concerns are shared during worship, the congregations pray for the needs of their neighbors in and out of the churches.

For the "always small" church to be healthy, it needs a spirit that welcomes constant improvement. These churches are unlikely to be receptive of an idea that challenges them to enter into a radically different future. Every few years some outsider—perhaps a recently arrived pastor or a judicatory official in the city—tries to excite them about merging their congregations and building a new centrally located church. Over the past sixty years they have learned well how to resist such ideas. But, these same people are extremely open to anything that will help them progress in their goal of making disciples for Christ. Constant improvement is for them a reasonable approach to the Christian life.

"Always small" churches also need to be part of a larger network. It is unlikely that these five churches would have survived if they had not had the larger parish for support. More than just being a means for providing a pastoral compensation package, the larger parish provides an outward looking window for churches, which, left to themselves, would hide behind their own stained glass. Because some of their fellowship events, as well as the well-attended weekly Bible study, are done together as a parish, the people have close Christian relationships outside of their individual congregation. This makes the average member of one of these small churches less provincial in their mind-set and more willing to do mission than a similar member of a mid-sized or larger church.

Beyond Numbers to Ministry

Let us define the small membership church in a way to focus on the problems shared by these churches and the successful adaptations they have made to their environment. Here is a more functional definition:

> A small church is any site with a worshiping congregation, whose normal income (this means routine offerings) and reasonable long-term expectation of worshiping congregation size, is insufficient to support the denomination's minimum compensation for an ordained pastor.

This definition would include in the small church category those churches that currently fund their ordained pastor by drawing on endowments, mission grants, or special outside contributions. It excludes from the small church category those congregations that are temporarily being served less than full-time because of an unusual circumstance, such as interim situations, as well as new church starts, which are planted with the expectation of becoming larger churches. Those denominations that have lower clergy compensation costs, would, by this definition, have a lower demarcation line between their small and mid-sized church categories.

Every church within this small church category faces a common set of problems as they attempt to survive and to serve and witness to their faith. The one universal and indispensable key to small church stability and health is to have the appropriate pastor. By "pastor," I mean the person who oversees the spiritual direction of the congregation, not necessarily the person who preaches most Sundays. In shared ministries this person may be variously called "lead pastor," "supervising elder," or "minister of administration." This person may be the sole clergy overseeing several small congregations or one of several clergy providing oversight to a group of churches. This person may be bi-vocational or part-time pastor. The concept of being one who oversees or supervises is an integral part of what it means to be the pastor of a small church today. Pastors of healthy small congregations do not do all the acts of ministry; they build a team that engages in ministry. The healthy small membership church claims its own ministry and looks to clergy for support.

To be an appropriate pastor for the small church, the person who serves the small church must commit to two areas of responsibility:

- Doing first that which needs to be done to equip the team for ministry, even if that seems contrary to the stated expectations of the congregation or the denominational authorities.

- Staying in one location long enough to develop close relationships and become an integrated part of the congregation.

The overseeing tasks of the local pastor, in addition to the two essential traits listed above, are logical outgrowths of defining the small church as incapable of supporting the "normal" one pastor-one church model. When small congregations are encouraged to claim their own ministries and look to their clergy for guidance, then they become better than the "normal" church and much closer to what Paul envisioned for the church when he wrote:

> It was he [Christ] who gave some to be apostles, some to be prophets, some to be evangelists, and some to be pastors and teachers, to prepare God's people for works of service, so that the body of Christ may be built up until we all reach unity in the faith...
>
> (Ephesians 4:11-13 NIV)

There is what some fear to be a blurring of the distinction between lay and clergy in the teamwork of the small church. The "works of service" come from a faith organization in which there is an expectation of unity rather than a division of roles between clergy and laity. In shared ministry situations (larger parishes, group ministries, cooperative clusters), a lay person may receive only a few weeks of formal training and then engage in pastoral work. If the shared ministry is rightly established, an ordained clergyperson supervises this lay person. Clergy remain responsible for the ongoing training of laity for ministry. This lay pastor brings to the job the rich experience of being nurtured for ministry in the context of that parish. Even for small church situations that do not utilize non-ordained pastors, the gap between clergy and lay is bridged in a way that distinctly honors the reformation principle of the priesthood of all believers (see 1 Peter 2:9).

The Attendance vs. Compensation Graph

The small congregation's lack of financial resources and numerical status means that it must seek creative means to obtain supervising pastors. Even in denominations that have an appointment system, such as the United Methodist Church, the clergy supply situation needs understanding by the lay leadership of the small congregation, so that they can proactively adapt to changes in the system. The small church Pastor Parish Relations Committee (or in other churches, the search committee) needs to be intentional about a team leader to fill the role of pastor. Unlike the mid-sized church, which has the luxury of receiving a "normal" ordained pastor out of the middle of an appointment pool, the small church must actively work the system with a sense of their own self-interest. To do anything less permits the denominational leadership to lapse into a patronizing role, that is, "trust us, we know what is best for you." I am not saying that denominational leaders in any way fail to do their jobs prayerfully and with a high degree of personal integrity. I have the highest respect for the people who hold those difficult offices, and each year I am amazed by the spiritual discernment and the willingness to respond appropriately to conflict by the bishop and cabinet of my own conference. But any human organization will fail to serve the weakest of its members, if those members do not find the courage to ask for what they need.

We live in interesting times. The number of mid-sized congregations who have become small by definition is dramatically increasing. Meanwhile the number of small churches who are biting the bullet and merging, closing, or sharing facilities with other congregation, is also on the rise. The social pressures driving this situation can be displayed with two simple graph lines.

- First, the costs of compensating an ordained full-time pastor increase at a rate that exceeds the general rate of inflation. The major cause of this rise is the cost of health insurance. Note also the rising cost of education (many recent seminary graduates have in excess of $100,000 in school loans) and the pension and salary adjustments approved during the good economy of the 1990s. Conferences, synods, or other judicatories cannot contain these costs, and it is unfortunate that many small church members blame the denomination for the bind that these rising costs place on their budget.

- The second line represents falling average worship attendance in small and mid-sized churches. For many churches this line has been steadily declining since 1970. Lower attendance always impacts the resources of the local church, and we cannot ignore the ways that this effects the budget.

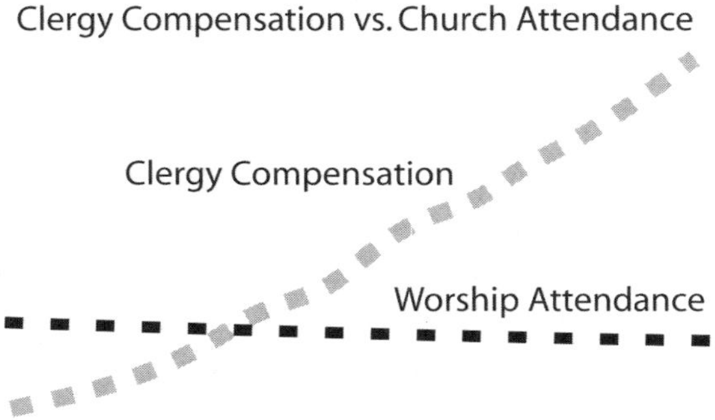

On the graph, the two lines cross and separate to reflect the effect this has upon the clergy supply system. Five years ago, most denominational officials worried about an expected clergy shortage. My own conference issued a statement that for a church to be served by an ordained clergy, the church should have at least one hundred in worship and two hundred on their membership rolls. Today it is becoming rare for a congregation of a hundred to afford their own pastor without significantly curtailing their programs, building maintenance, and mission giving. Meanwhile attendance steadily declines, and the average church is nowhere near the conference's standard expectation. The separation of these two lines will continue to make the demand for ordained clergy fall below the supply. The only mediating factor has been the number of clergy who are retiring early or departing the ministry because of burnout and discouragement about ministry.

If denominations fail to address the burnout issue, the systems will continue to pay the price in terms of rising healthcare costs, incidences of clergy misconduct, and the loss of effective leadership. If we become more sensitive to clergy health (a movement I optimistically see afoot in my own denomination), then the average retirement age will increase as pastors, like the rest of the population, find themselves feeling energized by their ministry well into their seventies. Already we are seeing many second-career clergy extend their service beyond the normal retirement age, and projected changes to the Social Security system are likely to encourage this. We may never experience the expected retirement bubble (the exit of pastors who were ordained in the 1960s), or at least it will be mitigated by the rapid drop in congregations who can afford an ordained pastor.

Taking Action

For the next decade we should see an oversupply of ordained clergy and an under-supply of lay pastors who have been trained to serve the small church. The denominational leadership, particularly those systems who provide guaranteed placement for their clergy, need to intentionally set about the following tasks:

- Provide suitable exit support for those clergy who no longer wish to serve in ministry. The money paid out in counseling, severance packages, and housing down payments will seem cheap when compared with the costs of keeping excess clergy in the system.

- Aggressively defrock those who lack the competence to pastor. No longer can we afford to tie continued ordination to keeping up with one's continuing education requirements or by avoiding charges of misconduct. The mid-sized and smaller churches need clergy with people skills. This soft quality may be hard to evaluate, but if our system moves away from its predilection to consider the rights of the individual clergy and instead considers the needs of parishes, we will reap rich benefits.

- Resist the urge to freeze or reduce clergy compensation. This is a knee jerk reaction to the social pressures listed and displayed in the graph above. If we do not adequately compensate the effective clergy who remain in the field, we will not have the heart to weed out those who are ineffective.

- Encourage current seminarians to consider specialized ministries and make the transition to appointments beyond the local church easier for all clergy.

- Provide transitional support for churches who are exploring shared ministries or relocation (see chapter 6). Implement the Partnerstep program designed by Ed Kail and Julia Kuhn Wallace (See *Partnersteps*, published by Discipleship Resources.) Interim ministers and congregational consultants will help lead churches to healthier clergy support arrangements.

- Track the number of full-time ordained clergy who are appointed each year to less than adequate situations and keep this figure in mind as decisions are made. If a pastor supervises fewer than 200 active members, are there other missional concerns that justify the placement? What is being done in the region to establish a shared ministry involving additional congregations?

- Encourage long term pastorates. Remove from ministry those who move from small church to small church because they lack the skills that are needed in the setting. Do everything possible to disrupt the existing career ladder that disparages multi-church settings in favor of the preferred one pastor-one church.

- Provide a range of appropriate training events for laity who wish to serve in some pastoral role. Develop suitable accreditation procedures and incentives for the variety of lay ministries.

The leadership of small churches need to confront the new reality being brought about by rising clergy compensation. If a church is currently joined with one or two other churches for the sake of making the minimum costs of an ordained clergy, they need to plan for a day when this arrangement will not be enough. If they are dependent upon a bi-vocational, retired, or student pastor, how long-term will this situation be? I do not write this to be alarmist, but to encourage interest in a process that supports all aspects of an effective small church pastoral ministry. To capitalize on the intimacy that marks the small membership church, pastoral leadership should stay long enough to develop trust. To reach out to their own neighborhoods for Christ, with the limited people and financial resources of the small church, the congregation needs clergy who will encourage the laity in ministry. With these as primary priorities, other attributes usually sought for in clergy become less important.

- While the small church needs a pastor who will teach them how to use their Bible effectively and encourage their leadership to use clear theological reasoning in their church work, the small church does not need a great preacher in their pulpit every Sunday. Effective lead pastors simply need to preach well enough to teach their lay speakers by example how to communicate their faith.

- While many small church members currently believe that it is their pastor's job to visit all of the sick and shut-ins, each congregation needs a compassionate and prayerful leader who will teach by example how to make an effective visit. The duty of the pastor is to organize those laity who have the spiritual gifts to visit the sick and shut-ins of the parish.

- While every congregation seeks for the magical minister who will make the church grow, this quest is misguided to the degree that it emphasizes the pastor's personal charisma. It is pointless to expect a new pastor to be so dynamic that she or he single-handedly brings back the disenchanted and fill the pews with young families and tithing professionals. Getting the pastor who looks like Jimmy Stewart and preaches like Peter Marshall will not bring the golden 1950s back to a dying small church. Instead of returning to the past, every small church needs a person who has the catalytic (not charismatic) ability to bring out the gifts and talents of the current membership.

The longer the current trends of rising clergy compensation cost and declining small church financial resources continue, the more general the rule that the only effective way to use ordained pastors in the small church is by having them supervise a large grouping of congregations in a shared ministry. This means that declining mid-sized churches and "once upon a time" small churches should give up on trying to afford their own pastor and actively seek to partner together with other churches. This means that churches who are currently yoked, or on circuits with one or two other churches, should think about including other congregations and forming larger regional ministries. As large shared ministries bring together groups of churches with one or two ordained pastors acting as supervising elders, then roles are opened up for indigenous laity to serve in a variety of pastoral roles. This achieves an economy of scale. The larger the grouping of churches, the more likely they will succeed. By *succeed*, I mean actively making disciples, both by the equipping of laity and by reaching out into the community.

The bonus to the whole process of transitioning churches into a shared ministry is that shared ministries provide such stable platforms for supporting their clergy's compensation packages that pastors are able to stay a very long time. There is no reason why a suitably trained and gifted clergy person or clergy couple could not spend their entire career supporting and developing the ministries of the congregations of one region. The churches also benefit from having a cluster of supporting congregations, who keep them accountable for doing their ministry in the context of their neighborhood. The word "context," meaning to "bloom where you are planted," is an important word for small church. Churches die when they get separated and lost from ministry to their own neighborhood. Having a covenant relationship with other churches in the region greatly increases a congregation's motivation to know and meet the needs of the community in their context.

This last definition of what it means to be a small membership church presents today's church leadership with three areas for intentional change.

First, both the currently small and the soon-to-be small church must redefine the leadership role and expectations they have of their pastor(s). Unlike what may be considered normal in their denomination, they have, or will soon have, some type of a "time share" clergy. They may share their pastor with other churches or with a mission project or with the pastor's other employment or with his or her retirement. Their pastor may be a student or a lay person engaged in some type of "on the job training" as they explore how to serve the church in new ways. These people blur the old separation between clergy and lay. The small church future does not need a clear distinction, only the formation of effective ministry teams.

Second, the church laity must be intentional about growing their own leadership skills to complement what they can no longer afford to purchase of an ordained pastor's time. Training laity to visit the shut-ins, lead committee meetings, teach, and preach makes sense not only in terms of economic survival, but in terms of the faithful stewardship of gifts entrusted to the community of faith. Christian ministry is far more joyful when one has the opportunity to serve in the area of one's spiritual gifts. Why should clergy have all the fun?

Finally, as the vast number of smaller congregations in every location actively seek a middle way between growth and stagnation, churches will encounter one another. Being intentional about sharing ministries and forming large cooperative relationships is the wave of the future. Smart churches will catch this wave early. They will explore a process, like *Partnersteps*, for initiating conversations between potential ministry partners. They will not wait until the crisis, but will start seeking partners today. They will not be afraid to cross any of the existing artificial boundaries or lines in seeking the best congregations to bring into the mix. The Holy Spirit will guide and sustain these small churches on the journey.

1 U.S. Census 2000 data. Each city's population hovered around 150,000.

Chapter Four

Will it Fly?

Bishop Jones had just spent a frustrating week at a conference where various church growth experts spoke about the cause of his denomination's membership loss. Church attendance is down, all agreed, but why? Some experts said that people no longer turn to the church for guidance on social or moral issues. Other used PowerPoint® graphics to prove how the younger generation is departing organized religion while, at the same time, expressing a deep yearning for true spirituality. His denomination's failure to embrace contemporary music and worship styles seemed to push them out of the mainstream of modern culture. Other church growth experts hammered home the statistical story that all across the country small membership churches are declining and dying, while large megachurches with their utilitarian buildings and organizational structure are growing. Bishop Jones turned to his wife and said, "I just spent four days being told that we need to get more people in the church." His wife smiled, barely looking up from her book, and raised an eyebrow as if to say, "Well, what did you expect?"

As they sat in the airport gate waiting area, the TV news carried a late-breaking story about an airplane crash. Investigators were dispatched to comb through the wreckage for clues. *Why did this happen?* Bishop Jones turned to his wife and said, "They don't need to do that. I know why that plane crashed." His wife arched her eyebrows again. "Every airplane crash is caused by the same thing," he went on, "Flying too close to the ground. If we could just keep planes from falling down, we'd be in luck."

"That's silly," his wife said.

The bishop knew it was silly, but the next day he said it again, this time to his staff. "I have just discovered why churches close. All churches die for the same reason. They have too few people." His staff lacked the courage to respond as honestly as his wife. If something is silly, why do we keep saying it?

Each year 3,500 to 4,500 congregations go out of existence.[1] One in five American congregations have lost more than 5% of their membership in the last five years.[2] Smaller and rural congregations are declining at significantly greater rates. Taken together these statistics, it is reasonable to predict that half of the current small churches will disappear in thirty years. Doing a statistical survey factoring in the age and life expectancy of our membership, and the marked failure we are experiencing in bringing the next generation into small church life, the prospect for the average small congregation looks bleak. This year we may feel lucky, as though we may beat the odds and share our church with the next generation. Every small congregation, though, intuitively senses how precarious their existence is. The exit of one major family or the discovery of a pastor's unethical behavior may put the church under. I know of one small country church that discovered that the field on which they parked every Sunday was owned by a new neighbor, who had plans for a high-priced development. In their 125-year history the need to own more land than what was needed to conduct worship and bury their dead had never occurred to this flock. It would be perhaps simplistic or silly to say that this church, like the other 1,500 churches which close each year, is imperiled because they didn't have enough people. But that is exactly what those who depart any small church on its last Sunday tend to say. Some will blame others: "The denomination made us close because we didn't have enough people."

For churches, the number of people attending worship or otherwise involved in the congregation's life is like the altitude of an airplane. Just as a plane will crash when it runs out of altitude, so also a church will die when it runs out of people. Investigating a plane crash to determine the cause involves looking at the series of events that led up to that loss of altitude. *What do the readings on each gauge and the records in the black box say about how the aircraft was functioning? Is there evidence on the cockpit recorder that the pilot was no longer in control? How were the pilot, crew, and maintenance staff functioning together as a system?* The goal of the investigation is safer air travel, and not simply to make planes fly higher. When we look at why churches are closing, we need to go beyond bemoaning the lack of people. It is also unsatisfying to say, "Well, a certain percentage of churches must close each year." What if the FAA (Federal Aviation Administration) took the same statistical view of an airplane crash? What if an aircraft investigator dismissed all crashes involving commuter turbo-props by saying, "Well you know, these small planes crash because they just aren't as safe as jumbo jets?"

With so many small churches failing, it is important to engage in some type of post-mortem investigation in the hope of developing congregational health and safety checklist. Church closures concern all of us. First, because those who have attended those churches have a deep emotional attachment to their congregational life and often fail to find other places to express their worship of God. Second, because other religious organization will not fill the vacancy left by these congregations. There is not in America a natural progression where churches are born, live a century or so, and then pass on their ministry to new congregations. What is lost in the death of a small church remains lost.

God calls the local church to make disciples of Christ in every available location. Consider the implications of Jesus' great commission, "go make disciples of ***all*** nations," (Matthew 28:19 NIV) and Jesus' final words to his disciples, "be my witnesses in Jerusalem, and in ***all*** *Judea* ***and Samaria***, and to the ends of the earth" (Acts 1:8 NIV). I believe that we are called to create and maintain disciple-making organizations in all places, even in social settings where it is difficult to be the church. A denomination with a diversity of church sizes is better equipped to maintain a witness for Christ in all parts of the culture and in all climates of public opinion--in the same way that an airline with a variety of planes can operate in all markets. To repeat one of the major themes of this book, small churches have the capability to operate in social contexts and neighborhoods that cannot support larger churches.

One further counterintuitive correlation between airplane crashes and church closures: what we need to fix is not always obvious. In WW II, Allied airplane manufacturers sent design engineers to the runways to examine the wounded planes that limped back after action. Often a bomber would have a gaping hole in its wing or fuselage or even an entire section of its tail missing. The engineers would carefully note the location of the damage and then go back and design reinforcements for future aircraft. The counterintuitive trick, though, was that they did not reinforce where they had seen damage, but rather where the planes were untouched. The logic was that the all the planes they looked at were survivors. Despite their extensive damage, these airplanes returned because they had not been hit in a vital spot. One can assume that the planes that did not return were hit in other places. Those other places were what needed reinforcement. By reinforcing where the surviving planes were untouched, the designers were taking into account the silent witness of those planes that didn't make it back because they were mortally wounded in other, more vital, places. So the counterintuitive rule was, "fix what you don't see broken, because what you do see broken isn't what causes airplanes to crash."

When experts from growing churches point to the successful programs and ministries of their church, they do not help the leaders of declining churches. Struggling congregations do not need to reinforce their ministries in the areas that growing churches are doing well. They need instead to reinforce the basic and vital areas of church life. Even individual people learn more from hearing someone share their failures than by hearing about someone's success. If you are a small church leader, don't focus on the success stories of those churches that are flying high above the need to worry about survival. Instead, study why churches like yours close. Do the post mortem; each closure includes a lesson about health in the congregation. To turn around a failing congregation may require a counterintuitive trick, a reinforcement of something that you previously may have thought unimportant. Like an airplane, a church is complex system of interdependent components. Understand the relationship between each of these components with an intent to find out what makes the small congregation survive and grow healthy.

Look at the frustration experienced by our fictional bishop in the opening of this chapter. He spent four days hearing things that were of little value to half of his congregations. Struggling small churches do not need reinforcement in the places where large churches have been successful. Our bishop is aware of many congregations that are successfully ministering in their context and making disciples, even though their attendance figures paled in comparison to the jumbo-jet expectations of the church growth consultants. The bishop is painfully aware of the many congregations who have tried every new program offered by his staff and yet, the pastors and laity can not gel as a team. Scores of his churches have become lifeless gatherings, failing to nurture their own spiritual growth and unable to reach out in a significant fashion to their communities. Some churches were in immediate danger of losing altitude and closing. Many, perhaps half, of the smaller churches nurture the perception that the denomination has let them down; these churches take on the role of victim.

The vital relationship between the local church and the greater church is becoming dysfunctional in more and more places. These churches are like airplanes flying for an airline and failing to do the necessary maintenance and refueling. If the basic support structures are unsound, how can even the best pilot assure his or her passengers of safety? Further, what can the pilot (pastor) and crew (local lay leadership) of one airplane do if the airline provides such poor customer service that no one wants to fly with them? It is hard to find anything in the church growth literature that will turn around a church that feels like it has been let down by its own denominational structure.

Programs such as the Church Vitality Indicator or Natural Church Development take a different approach by providing tools for analyzing a congregation's drivers for ministry or its weakest area. These tools provide valuable aid in understanding where a church is likely to fail and what needs healing within a congregation. In what follows we will continue to use the airplane metaphor to look at the essential relationships and structures that need to work well for the small church to fly. By doing this we will ignore the gaping holes (where a church fails to look the way church growth experts say it should look), which every small church has. We will concentrate on reinforcing those things, which if missing, will cause the church to crash and burn.

Low Fuel

Every airplane has a fuel gauge--often two or three. Just like our cars, an idiot light comes on when the gas is low. Plenty of airports with refueling facilities are scattered throughout the country. And yet every year, a number of planes, (usually small ones, run out of fuel and need to make emergency landings. This may seem silly until we remember, with embarrassment, the last time we ran out of gas in our family car.

The fuel that a small church cannot run without is spiritual passion. Spiritual passion motivates ministry. It shows in the congregation's answer to the question, "What excites you about Jesus?" If the person in the pew does not see a connection between faith and excitement, then the church is running on fumes.

The following factors indicate a congregation's spiritual passion tank:

– Constant Prayer

– Inspiring Worship

– Biblical Literacy

– An Emphasis on Faith as "Good News"

– A Conviction That People Need the Lord

– A Desire to Share Faith with Others

When a church is running out of gas, that is, when it lacks spiritual passion, the people think of their faith as a private matter. They rarely tell their neighbors that they even attend a church; they do not seek to share Jesus with neighbors. Worship gets in a rut. It feels dull, predictable, and safe. The congregation may believe that the Bible is important, but they also believe that the Bible is beyond understanding. Its power is drained away by a perception that the Bible lacks relevance. In the low passion church, religious language is couched in ambiguity and opposing points of view are held together with Christ. Little happens to motivate the people to rise above mediocrity in the Christian walk.

This condition is unrelated to the church's theological position or its denominational identity. Small churches with evangelical or fundamentalist creeds can have low spiritual passion. The condition is not related to the style of worship; simply singing praise choruses will not rescue a church that is running on fumes. The problem is more closely tied to whether those who are active in the congregation perceive that the church offers truth that is relevant and worth sharing with others. A burned-out pastor may drain more spiritual life from the church than he or she contributes, but the root cause of low spiritual passion usually lies deeper than the current minister.

Poor stewardship is also a frequent indicator of low spiritual passion in a church. People tend to give sacrificially to causes about which they feel passionate. It is not guilt, but rather a sense that what they are doing together as a congregation has day-to-day relevance, which leads people to consistently give. Stewardship programs will not lift the church's financial health, if the church does not address first its lack of spiritual passion.

Reluctance to spend time in prayer is another indication of a congregation with low spiritual passion. The congregation with sufficient spiritual passion is constantly in prayer for the needs of their non-churchgoing neighbors. In lifting the prayer needs of others they will often remark, "How can they go through what they are going through without faith?" But the congregation low on passion simply names the members who are sick, and members complain if the pastor prays "too long" or includes periods of silence in worship. For the people of a church running on empty, prayer is a ritual act, done with certain words at certain times and having little relevance to life. For the people of a spiritually passionate church, prayer is the center of their religious life. They do not need a pastor to remind them when to pray; they insist n prayer at every gathering.

If a church is low on spiritual passion, then it needs to openly admit it and address this area. It is as serious as an airplane running out of fuel. Often pastors and other church leaders feel reluctant to admit their inability to communicate their own spiritual intensity to the rest of the congregation. This common denial makes it convenient to think that a congregation's spiritual passion is a factor somehow beyond our control. Some specific actions can be prescribed for congregational spiritual health:

First, re-establish prayer as the central facet of church life. When Jesus cleansed the temple, he acted out of a commitment to restore that house of worship with Solomon's original purpose for the building: that it be "a house of prayer" (2 Chronicles 6:19-40 , Isaiah 56:7, Matthew 21:13). In many places the basic practice of prayer must be re-taught. People need to pray for their own needs and to spend time in intercession for one another. Begin by spending an entire season of worship, such as Lent, focused on prayer. At the end of this extended period of teaching, leaders may more easily identify members of the congregation with the spiritual gift of intercession because they will be the most energized. Organize this group to keep the congregation, its ministries, missionaries, and leaders constantly lifted in prayer. Take time also to evaluate the personal prayer life of the church leadership. How does it need to be strengthened? If leadership are not serious about prayer, it is unlikely that others will become passionate about prayer.

Re-shape worship so that it will be more inspiring. The size of a congregation is not an excuse for mediocre worship. Each service of worship needs appropriate preparation. It should have clearly stated theme, and care should be taken to limit ambiguity, miscommunication, jargon, and any perceptions of fuzziness. Inspirational worship is hard to achieve when those who lead it lack conviction about their faith. Just as a garden needs to be weeded from time to time, the liturgy and ritual may need to be re-examined through congregational study. As with prayer, basics of Christian faith may need to be recovered. Leaders may need to deal with assumptions about worship, such as why we worship God. Good small church worship is profoundly simple without being childish. Music does not need to sound like recordings, but music should be done well. Leaders should discern how the music will connect with the heart of the congregation. People are most receptive to having worship inspire them when familiar acts of worship are balanced by challenging new insights. If a congregation suffers from low spiritual passion, then it is not the time for those leading worship to force their musical taste on those in the pew nor is it safe to continue doing the same old thing. The questions to ask are essential: "What will lead to more enthusiasm among those who participate in this service? What will lead people to deeper awareness of Christ? What will enable people to become open to God?"

Promote biblical literacy. "Why should my faith excite me?" is a question that underlies spiritual passion, The Bible answers that question on page after page in the stories of people who lived by faith, and it instructs us in how we can live for God. I am convinced that reading the Bible releases passion in a Christian's life. The method, the translation, or even the study program is not as important as opening the Bible and reading it. People simply need to read the Bible every day. To do that the church needs easy-to-understand Bibles in the homes of each of its members. American Bible Society (americanbible.org) and the International Bible Society (ibsdirect.com) both sell inexpensive Bibles by the case. One of the churches that I served needed to get rid of its old King James pew Bibles. We asked people in the congregation to consider purchasing both a Bible in memory or honor of a loved one for their pew and one for their home. At the same time we challenged the congregation to read through the entire Bible. There are one- and three-year plans available, which break the Bible into daily readings. Since the idea of donating towards the purchase of pew Bibles was well received, the church was also able to purchase additional Bibles to give to others.

A congregation's biblical literacy also depends upon the attitude the leaders of study groups have when they present the Scriptures. If the pastor or Sunday school class leader prefaces every remark with the caution, "We are not really sure what this means...," then people get the impression that the Bible is irrelevant and incomprehensible. Leaders must enjoy making the Scriptures clear to the community of faith, so the people will grow in their awareness of God's grace.

Finally, don't be afraid to ask and re-ask the question, "Why aren't we excited about our faith?" If people respond, "But we are," then the next question is, "Why don't you tell others about your faith?" The willingness to be public about one's faith is the litmus test of spiritual passion. When a couple begins to date, if one of the parties is less inclined to tell others about the relationship, it is an indicator that they are not feeling energized by that relationship. No matter what one person says to another in private, what they proclaim in public reveals passion. The more honestly a congregation can wrestle with their own reluctance, the clearer the attitudes and people that are blocking enthusiasm. Ask this question, "How would Jesus respond to our church? Would he see us as passionate or lacking passion?"

Being without spiritual passion does not make a church a bad church; it only makes it a dying church. If we return to the analogy of the FAA investigating an airplane crash, we can picture a chain of events that caused the accident. An airplane might have been on a routine flight, but then encountered bad weather and had to circle the airport to which they were heading. Then a decision was made to change destinations. In the process of flying to the next city, the pilot got lost. Eventually the airplane ran out of fuel and crashed. One could blame weather, bad directions, mechanical failure, pilot error, and low fuel for the eventual accident, but of these causes, the fuel should have been honestly appraised early and kept in mind each step of the way. Every aircraft is designed with a sufficient fuel tank for its range.

Every small church, like the airplane, is appropriately designed to maintain the spiritual passion of its membership. Conflict and poor pastoral leadership may drain the passion from a church, but the community shares actual responsibility. The responsibility also extends beyond the community to the systems (for example, economic, demographic, denominational) in which the church participates.

The final action of our Lord in establishing the church was to send the Holy Spirit on Pentecost. The Spirit is more than just our personal comforter or even a provider of spiritual gifts to the leadership of the church. The Holy Spirit is also the gift of fire to ignite the passion of the congregation. The Book of Acts describes not just the work of the apostles (or clergy), but also the ways all the believers gave attention to prayer, teaching, and the study of the scriptures. During this period each congregation was small in size, but rich in enthusiasm. They did not worry about their membership being apathetic or more committed to sports or shopping than to Christian faith. If in our own era we feel a bit distant from this experience, we should remember the promise Jesus made when he said,

> "If you then, though you are evil, know how to give good gifts to your children, how much more will your Father in heaven give the Holy Spirit to those who ask him!"
>
> (Luke 11:13 NIV)

Refueling a congregation's fuel tank is a process that involves the confession of our need and the seeking for a general outpouring of God's spirit. Many evangelism programs and study books can guide congregations recover interest in the Holy Spirit, but the key to inviting the passion back into the life of a congregation lies with the basics: prayer, scripture study, and the uncompromised profession of God's glory in worship.

Getting Lost

The airplane pilot interrupts the flight and announces to his passengers that he has some good news and some bad news. The bad news is that they are lost. The good news is they have a good tail wind and are making great time.

For airplanes, as well as for small churches, getting lost is no joking matter. A pilot disoriented by poor visibility may easily crash the plane into a mountain. Before adequate aircraft instrumentation, it was not unusual for a pilot to fly into a cloudbank right side up and exit the cloud upside down. Flying by the seat of one's pants is not what it is cracked up to be. Being in the wrong place at the wrong time can be fatal. In September of 1983, 269 people died when a Korean Airlines 747 en route from Alaska to South Korea drifted into Soviet airspace and was shot down by Russian air defense. I suspect that many small churches have died because they were unaware of their context and the direction their ministries needed to take to be relevant to their neighborhood.

Airplane pilots can become disoriented in two ways; they can fail to understand their direction (and from this, their place on the map) or they can mistake their altitude relative to the terrain (height above the ground). Churches can mistake their purpose (direction), and hence misunderstand their unique place in their region's religious landscape. They also can become disconnected from their people and fail to gain the new members they need to continue. In most aircraft, the importance of not getting lost is underscored by the placement of two large instruments in the middle of the console. The altimeter shows the current height of the airplane above sea level. The altimeter is often flanked by additional instruments, showing height relative to the ground as well as the rate of climb or fall. The other large instrument is the compass, which shows not only direction and also whether or not one is flying on the level. These instruments along with accurate maps have become an indispensable part of air travel; flying "by the seat of the pants" is not acceptable for any pilot. In the church, it is irresponsible to attempt to operate without being aware of one's statistics and the local demographics. Lay leadership and clergy need to survey the needs of the church's neighborhood and to reflect upon how people find the church and enter into the life of the congregation. Questions to ask include: *What is this church's unique purpose? How do statistics, such as the number of people joining or the weekly worship attendance, reflect recent actions of the church? How can we keep these numbers and the need to reach new people always before our congregation?*

Lost churches exhibit the following problems:

The average person in the pew on Sunday morning will look very different from the people who live near the church. The congregation may contain only older adults, but kids fill the parking lot with games of hopscotch during the week. The church reflects a homogeneous social class or ethnicity that is not common in the surrounding area. The church has traditionally ministered to a particular group, which is now moving out of the neighborhood, and the people have few contacts in the transitional area. The church offers few, if any, activities and programs that encourage members to meet the new people.

A reluctance to try new things shows much. If you don't know where you are, you will be reluctant to get off of the beaten path. The congregation that seems fixed in its attitude may be reeling from a social disorientation.

The church leadership, including the pastor, cannot name anyone with whom they are currently trying to share faith. Further, they cannot name people who they know are not disciples. The church has built an intimate fellowship, which shields people from having to make friends in the world.

The church has few or no programs that make contact with or meet the needs of non-Christians.

New Christians, or even people who have not been raised in the church, find the jargon of the worship service and church publications intimidating. Little effort is made to communicate with those who haven't always been a part of this church.

People of the church no longer think creatively about ways to share Christ in the neighborhood. Years of church council meetings show no evidence of doing anything for evangelism.

Newcomers are not made to feel welcome. The congregation thinks it is friendly, but members are friendly only to to other members. The laity leave the job of getting to know visitors to the pastor.

Despite pulpit pronouncements, the sense in the pew is one becomes a Christian by being born to Christian parents. Laity do not talk about faith as a decision and a commitment one makes.

Groups who rent the church facility do not see or hear anything that invites them to consider the church for their religious needs. The use of the church by outsiders is not seen as an opportunity to invite those people to become insiders.

One of the questions I sometimes ask church leaders is, "How does this church differ from the Lions Club or the Grange Hall down the street (or whatever social organization is present in the community)?" People give a variety of answers, often centered upon the church's activities. They talk about how the church has worship, Sunday school, a Bible study, a prayer circle. They point to how these "good for you" things differ from the entertainment focus of the local social club. I will, if possible, point out how worthy the activities of the particular social group are. Eventually someone will say, "Well, we believe in Christ." This gets them a little closer, but I still challenge them by pointing out that the social clubs also have principles that they affirm. It often takes the members of a small church a long time to arrive at a unique purpose for their church that justifies all the work that they do. The purpose of the church is to offer Christ to those who need him. Jesus said, "...go and make disciples of all nations, baptizing them in the name of the Father and of the Son and of the Holy Spirit, and teaching them to obey everything I have commanded you" (Matthew 28:19-20 NIV). To use the compass analogy, this is the true north, which guides every small church across a changing and disorienting social landscape. If the people of a church become so busy doing what they think they should be doing that they forget this central command; they are lost. For a church, being lost can be fatal.

Jesus used the word *lost* to describe those people who were in need of a new relationship with God. In the pivotal fifteenth chapter of Luke, Jesus tells three stories in a row, each about something or someone who is lost. In each of these parables, Jesus stresses both the desperate need of the one who is lost and the purposeful actions of the one who finds. The last of these stories tells of a young man who becomes lost from his moral values and his home. The father, the seeker of the lost, meets this prodigal boy with clothing, honor, and a meal. The father has obviously thought ahead about what the boy would need upon his return.

This last parable in Luke 15 symbolizes the type of evangelism the people in a healthy small church do week in and week out. They study the needs of their community and try to think what they have to offer that will so connect with those needs that people will be brought home to the love of God. A small church in an inner city neighborhood might offer meals and clothing in addition to a compassionate fellowship that openly embraces the people of their street. The small church in a more middle class rural area might have a senior fellowship lunch, which shows honor and concern to each person who enters. Another small church uses a major portion of its prayer circle meeting to pray by name for the people the members know who do not have faith in God. One small church in a county seat rents a booth at the fair each year. The members pass out free bottled water and have a shady spot for people to sit and rest. Each of the lay people who work that booth are willing to pray and speak a few honest, comforting, words of faith to anyone who asks. They are careful to avoid overly assertive or preachy remarks; they simply and eloquently share good news. On the trendy south side of Pittsburgh a small church holds a Bible study in a local tattoo parlor. They get a lot of mileage out of talking about Jesus as one who was "pierced for our sins." In each of these situations the church's evangelism is shaped to conform to the needs to the people surrounding the church.

The church that is willing to ignore the needs of those who have not yet found a loving congregation is a church that has lost its own understanding of the heart of Jesus. The church that does not engage in some purposeful action to seek the lost within its neighborhood is a church that has chosen to ignore its own spiritual compass. The church, however, that has recovered the true meaning of the word *evangelism* (to share good news), is paying attention to its compass. When the church goes the second mile to discover the needs of those in its neighborhood, then it is diligently studying the map so that it does not stray again. The concept of need-oriented evangelism is an important one for small church survival.

Good pilots watch their altimeter. The definition of flying involves staying above the ground, and the definition of being a church involves having people together in a fellowship. In an airplane, the number of feet above sea level is a statistic, a number we rejoice that someone is watching. In the church, the number of people actively involved (active members) is also an important statistic. Some airplanes have a smaller gauge beside the altimeter labeled "rate of climb" (which also measures how fast you are falling). Churches, especially small churches, need to be aware of their own rate of climb--whether they are gaining or losing members.

What is important is not just absolute altitude, but the altitude relative to the terrain. 10,000 feet seems like a safe cruising height, unless you are flying over the Andes. How many people are enough people? Well, that depends on where you are the church. Every church has a context, and that context determines the number of people needed in worship in order for that church to fly. If that church is ministering in the context of a growing suburb with rising home values, then that number is likely to be quite high. Why? The people of that upwardly mobile setting will place a high value on quality music, ministerial credentials, and the church's appearance. When the choir is a few struggling voices, the preacher looks homespun, and the building lacks functioning air-conditioning, these same neighbors who bypass the dollar store will bypass the church. Small churches have a hard time in some contexts, and to fly in these places, they need to gear their efforts to meet the qualities that are expected. Fortunately, most small churches are in less demanding contexts. They can do well with fewer people, because they meet the needs of neighbors who are seeking for other qualities. An extreme example is that of congregations in recreational areas, which often need to learn how to fly well with a congregation of the few year-round residents in order to be open to minister during the peak season.

Small churches affirm that size is not an indication of greatness. Some churches with only a few dozen on their membership rolls have a close Christian fellowship and offer a consistent witness to Christ by their loving deeds in the community. They intuitively know how to relate what they are doing to the great commission Jesus gave to his disciples in the mountain in Galilee (Matthew 28:19-20). Other churches may have hundreds of members, but may be clueless as to why Jesus would want those people on the roll of his church. They are seriously lost. Congregations can drift from their mission and still remain happy and well-attended. It is possible to make a wrong turn and drive blissfully many miles in the wrong direction, not realizing that we are lost. But eventually there comes the rude awakening that we are lost. The tough lesson of our current era of declining church attendance is that religious organizations cannot afford to drift too long. Society always calls to reckoning those institutions that have a good time, but fail to meet a serious need.

Structural Problems

If you have accumulated frequent flyer miles, you have probably experienced the "delay due to mechanical problems." The plane may sit on the tarmac and passengers have fastened seat belts, and then you see out the window those mechanics and technicians in blue coveralls. They gesture and look puzzled. They probe various trap doors and crevices in the plane's wing with their meters and other tools. Minutes drag by until the pilot comes on the intercom with an apology and asks everyone to deplane. Your mind races through the consequences of missed connections and your stomach flip flops with anger, but actually you should gush with joy and relief. A mechanical delay surely beats losing an engine at 30,000 feet.

The point is not just that airplanes, with their physical complexity, frequently require repair. Airlines have procedures for inspection and maintenance, which are vital for passenger safety. The money needed to keep an airplane airworthy is an indispensable part of the budget. Further, replacement of aging aircraft and regular upgrading of planes and facilities is considered the cost of doing business. Investments may be deferred, but never ignored altogether.

Unlike airplane owners, many congregations engage in a penny wise and pound foolish neglect of their facilities. They may keep their carpet clean and their pews polished, but they tolerate week after week an inadequate sound system or they fail to salt the walk on icy days. They may voice a concern about the quality and longevity of their pastors, but they pass a yearly budget that neglects to maintain the pastor's housing. From time to time, the entire church building or parsonage will need replacement. This decision can be deferred, but it cannot be ignored.

The airline analogy teaches us that the physical affects the spiritual. The best church buildings in the world will not bring to life a dying congregation. Often the idolatrous love of the building contributes to a church's demise. An airplane may be in tip-top mechanical shape, but still run out of gas or get lost. The physical form, or building, in which a congregation lives must support the ministries and life of that church. It provides the expected amount of comfort for the spiritual journey. It has to seat the right number of people and include a place for their luggage (the church parking lot needs to be adequate), without being overly large or wasteful of fuel. It has to inspire confidence without being ostentatious. The plane must sit at the correct or scheduled airport and gate when the passenger shows up, which relates to the church building's location. This discussion relates to the concept of scalability, stewardship, and a congregation's character. Does this fellowship have the wisdom, generosity, and courage, to do what is needed for its earthly home?

A new church start, because it began small, rented a series of facilities, including a school cafeteria that required them to set up the worship area and tear it down each weekend. All mid-week meetings occurred in people's homes. Their stuff was packed and unpacked from a van each Sunday. The pastor said, "Being a church in a box can be exhausting." As they grew, they constantly moved until they finally could afford to buy adequate land and build. What kept this church functioning and growing, besides a passionate spirituality, was the wise and courageous willingness to shape their outward form to meet their current need.

Another congregation is over a hundred years old and still has a lively ministry to the children of the community. Because they invited into their Sunday school many children who are from unchurched families, the children in the dank, small basement often outnumbered the forty or so adults who gathered for worship. The church was landlocked on a busy intersection, its front door practically opening on to the street. Teachers worried about the kids running out into traffic. One of the church members, a farmer, offered the church land to relocate. With a gutsy-ness rarely seen in small, older congregations, they accepted the land, built a new educational facility as a ground floor, and then moved their old sanctuary on top as a second story. The new facility successfully married their quaint worship space with the place they needed to be in order to continue their passion of reaching the children of the town.

These examples show the willingness to step back and objectively analyze the structures that support the congregation's life together and their particular outreach to the community. To fail to plan for regular inspection, maintenance, and review courts disaster. To lack the courage and the generosity to make radical changes when necessary guarantees obsolescence, which in the case of a church, means slow death. These structures actually come in three forms:

First, and most obvious are the buildings and property that house the worship, program life, and, if there is a parsonage, pastoral leadership of the congregation. Unhealthy churches let their buildings determine their actions. They shy away from ministries because they want to protect their building. They continue to gather each week in a too large sanctuary, oblivious to how uninviting and cold it makes their worship feel. Healthy churches shed what they no longer need, like a snake sheds its old skin. Healthy churches think first about their purpose of making disciples in their context, and then shape the facility to match.

Second comes the decision-making structure that organizes the church's programmatic life. Unhealthy churches will have some combination of the following problems:

> A few people, or sometimes one person, autocratically make all the decisions. The remainder of the congregation feels left out.
>
> No clear process for making decisions is in place. An idea gets tossed from person to person, and no one feels that they have the authority to decide. The church is paralyzed because it lacks a clear pathway for decisions.
>
> The church waits for outside people and events to make decisions for them. They expect the denomination or the pastor to tell them what to do. They wait for things to break, and then they fix them.
>
> Isolated groups make decisions without consulting with other groups. If the church kitchen needs remodeling, either the trustees or the women's society care for the job, but neither group will talk with the other about their desire. Neither group will consider the interests of the daycare group, which also uses the facility.

No matter how small a church is, it needs a working decision-making structure. Small churches should carefully design and implement a leadership rotation policy, stating how long people can stay in offices such as council chair, trustee board, and financial secretary. It is important that the people develop these term limits rather then simply copy them from denominational guidebooks. When democracy was first developed in ancient Greece, government officials were chosen by lot, and rarely served for more than a year. For these very small city-states, authority was not seen as something given only to those with the most friends and influence; authority was a civic duty at which every citizen took a turn. In the small church, with its emphasis on loving relationships, the concept of everyone taking a turn in office works well. The leaders facilitate the group in making decisions, rather than telling people what to do. The structure (how things get decided) needs to be clearly charted. Each decision-making group is responsible to write down procedures and processes and to share this information with the new group or committee members. Paradoxically, having clear understanding of where the authority of each group lies helps groups to consult with one another.

The third form of structure involves volunteer placement. If the membership of a church is nurtured into active discipleship by their participation in the church, then some mechanism should connect each individual with areas of service that match their own talents, temperament, and spiritual gifts. In most small churches, the pastor plays a pivotal role in inviting people to consider new areas of service. He or she does this not only by leading the nomination or lay leadership committee, but also by the weekly communication of new opportunities for volunteers. If the pastor performs this task joyfully, tactfully, and with a sincere interest in seeing the laity expand their practice of faith, it is amazing how much the witness of the whole congregation can be strengthened. Many pastors state that this process is one of their least favorite aspects of ministry. As I reflect upon why I feel this way, I realize that it is because of my reluctance to delegate or ask for help. It seems easier for me to do certain things rather than to ask and train a lay person. I enjoy some forms of church work, and I have to tell myself not to be so selfish. This dangerous attitude must be held in check by constantly reminding myself that God has gifted people to serve. When a pastor is sensitive enough to discern where and how an individual might grow spiritually by being invited to do the task that matches their latent potential and then invites that person to consider the task, that personal connection might do more good for the church than a month of sermons.

A congregation can do several things to support the pastor in this process of volunteer placement.

Hold a congregation-wide spiritual gift study and inventory. This inventory should be repeated every other year, not only to capture new attendees, but to reinforce the concept that the Holy Spirit is actively gifting the people of the congregation.

Encourage everyone who has been doing a job for several years in the church to mentor someone else in this ministry. Good Sunday school teachers need to train and mentor future teachers. The treasurer needs to develop his or her replacement, even if they do not plan to step down any time soon. This process goes a long way towards preventing burnout and provides a low stress way for someone to experiment with a job before committing to it.

Throughout the year, not only at nomination time, share with the pastor and the lay leadership committee the latent gifts and hidden talents you have discovered in the people of the congregation. Pastors are often clueless about the untapped potential of their congregations.

Set the standard high for putting faith into practice. Let it be known that active membership in this congregation means not just giving money and showing up at worship, but also involves giving of one's time and skills.

Encourage the people to see their commitment to volunteer work outside of the church as a form of Christian service. When members are encouraged to give back to the community, they witness to Christ, which, even though it may not show up on statistical reports, richly blesses the witness of the congregation. Many churches celebrate a "Laity Sunday," which provides an occasion to honor the witness to faith the people do by their volunteer work in the community and by their faithfulness to Christ in their secular employment.

Healthy churches are perceived by their community as being bigger than their actual size because each individual in congregation has been brought by the structure to serve gladly with their gifts. A sense of teamwork marks the spirit of these congregations, and complaints of burnout are rarely heard. The congregation sticks to a decision-making process that works for them, and they refuse to let any individual or faction derail that process. Leaders rotate, serving three years or less, then move on to other tasks.

A healthy congregation's building may not look lavish or have a lot of spare rooms. It is, however, well maintained and each area is used by the programs that fit in that area. The congregation has a sense of stewardship, which prevents them from having rooms or pews remain unoccupied for long. The people have systems in place to review their facility needs. Their affection for their building does not prevent them from making objective choices about it.

Pilot Error

Very few major airliner crashes are caused by pilot error. Unfortunately many small civil airplanes are flown into trouble by their amateur pilots. Small churches are often seriously jeopardized by unsuitable pastors. Pastors can contribute to each of the problems listed in this chapter. But to be fair, it is extremely rare that a church's closing can be attributed to the incompetence of one clergy. Out of the relationship between pastor and parish there develop cycles of behavior, which may be both dysfunctional and un-Christian. These cycles may be self-perpetuating and extend long after the initiating pastor and key laity of the church have left.

It is also rare to be able to point to one single incident or failure in judgment and say that is where all the trouble began. Instead, patterns of miscommunication and abuse of authority are put into place piece by piece. Soon no person, no matter how wise and gentle, can arrive as the new pastor and have the level of trust necessary for the job. The congregation also loses the capacity to love each other in the forgiving fashion which they need to continue as an intimate small church.

We hear a common expression, "Be careful what you ask (or pray) for." Even in the denominational systems where the new pastor is appointed without much input from the church, congregations receive what they ask for rather than what they need. A church low on spiritual passion will gladly receive a pastor who has a lowered set of expectations regarding enthusiasm, commitment to stewardship, and the public witness of faith. When they run out of gas a few years later, the church blames the pastor. Churches that have lost their sense of purpose often ask for and receive pastors who have little interest in doing more than the minimum. The institution without a clue about purpose is married to a leader who has no sense of direction. They are happy together, even though their numbers dwindle year by year. They do not grasp the fact that people need a reason to belong to the church. A religious organization needs to be organized to go somewhere with its faith. Congregations disconnected from the culture of their neighborhood often ask for and receive pastors who share their myopic view. Churches at odds with their denomination are matched to pastors who have problems with authority. Patterns are perpetuated.

In terms of leadership style and pastoral skill, if the people on the search committee (or Pastor-Parish Relations committee) like the previous pastor, they will seek someone with the same qualities. They may talk among themselves about how the church needs to be led in a new direction, but when they meet with their denominational representative they ask for more of the same. If people are openly hostile towards their previous minister, they will have a hard time presenting a balanced profile. Instead of seeking a new person who will go forward, while bringing to the church their own mix of gifts and defects, they seek someone to erase the past.

The healthy congregation views each pastoral change as a transitional process. Part of that process includes grieving the loss of the previous pastor. Time needs to be provided to recognize in worship that even the best gifts of life are given only for a season and that the congregation will move on. If that relationship was not positive, the congregation still needs time to reflect and speak about what was learned and gained by the church under that ministry. The words from Shakespeare's *Julius Caesar*, "The evil which men do lives after them, their good is often interred with their bones," serves as a warning.[3] A congregation cannot move forward until it has laid to rest the ill feelings about the previous pastor. They also need to resurrect the good, by claiming the programs and leadership structures this person put into place. The healthy congregation then takes the time to come to know the new pastor as a distinct individual. They do not rush the relationship formation period of the change, but keep doing "get to know you" activities well into the second year.

Given all this, however, there are times when clergy fail the local church. Small churches are vulnerable to the following pastor-related problems:

Failure to meet reasonable work expectations. The effective small church pastor does not do the ministry, but rather equips others to do their ministry. This delegation of tasks and the oversight of the decision-making process of the congregation (attending meetings) requires a certain amount of pastoral presence. The pastor must give the time he or she promised to give when he or she committed to come to the situation. Small churches, by necessity, are remarkably resilient, adapting to share their pastor with other congregations or the pastor's secular employment. The important issue, however, is the covenant made and the mutual expectations each needs to be able to hold the other accountable to in order to build a foundation for trust. If the pastor takes his or her salary and fails to spend the time, or spends the time ineffectively doing nonessential tasks, he or she is committing theft. Sooner or later the congregation will feel cheated.

This type of pastor-related problem can be solved by the intervention of a denominational representative or a church consultant. A congregation's expectations of the pastor needs communication and should relate to the current compensation. If the two do not match, which expectations should be taken out of the job description? Is the pastor willing to commit more time to specific areas? Each party must recognize the need for negotiation. The pastor cannot volunteer or give more time than agreed to earlier nor can the church buy a full-time pastor with a part-time salary. Because it is hard to keep in these types of conversations on track, a mediator is very helpful. These meetings also need to occur soon or else conflict will threaten the pastor's ministry and the church's existence.

The pastor may be ill-suited for work in the small church. Because the small church pastor is often bi-vocational, retired from other employment, or newly trained for ministry, they are often seen as amateurs. The root of the word *amateur*, actually comes from the Latin word for love. It implies that the amateur is someone who does what they love. Even though small church pastors may not have a seminary education, they can be well suited if their love for the job drives them to constant learning. Theological competence and leadership skill may be learned in the parish if a person's heart is in the right place. The problem many small churches have is with pastors who learned only what they needed to get placed, and they have spent every moment since the completion of requirements in sharing their ignorance. Because small churches focus upon relationships, pastors need real people skills. Even people with seminary degrees may be ill-suited for the small church if they lack the capacity to listen. A small church is better off without a pastor than having a pastor who does not care for the people.

When a pastor is poorly suited for small church work, it is rarely a failure of education. Perhaps the pastor has become burned out or disenchanted with ministry. Perhaps the pastor has doubts about vocational calling and needs to explore that question. Such matters are worth exploring through some type of sabbatical leave. At minimum, a church must insist that the pastor take time off each week and participate in regular activities for spiritual renewal. Many clergy, however, need to seriously look at the indications that they may be temperamentally unsuited for small church ministry.

Pastors who can't seem to leave. Some pastors move on to another situation, but continue to officiate at weddings and funerals. Others retire and buy a home in the community so that they can be around to give free advice and stir up trouble. These busybodies do great harm. A trusting relationship needs to be established with the new pastor before the new pastor can make much headway in guiding the church forward. This process does not begin in a small church until it has fully said good-bye to the previous pastor. If the lay people can recognize how dangerous the situation is, then they might find the appropriate words to speak to the clergy who continues in an unofficial role in the community. If not, the tenure of the new pastor will not remain very long.

Clergy misconduct. Separate misconduct from the difficulties most pastors have when it is discovered that the minister's behavior does not meet the high standard of some of the congregation's members. A pastor may let slip an inappropriate word or engage in some other act of foolishness. Because he or she is the minister, the incident is tried in the gossip court of the small church. This is not misconduct. Misconduct involves behaviors that are markedly unethical, not just for clergy, but for anyone. These behaviors may be sexual in nature or they can involve emotional abuse or violence. There may be a larger pattern of the pastor overstating his or her authority. There may be victims who deserve an appropriate response from the congregation. Financial misconduct by clergy is also prevalent enough that every church should regularly audit the funds the pastor accesses. To return to the airplane analogy, this is when a pilot's error causes a mid-air collision. Casualties are likely to be high. The church may not fly again.

The steps churches need to take to prevent misconduct or to respond to allegations, are beyond the scope of this book (see *Safe Sanctuaries* by Joy Thornburg Melton, published by Discipleship Resources). Smaller congregations need to keep several concepts in mind:

> Misconduct causes congregational trauma. Some people will respond by rallying to the pastor's support. They may consider the whole investigation to be a sign of disloyalty to someone they have trusted. They may continue to keep faith in their pastor, no matter what evidence, and even to blame the victim. Others may quickly vilify the pastor and question why he or she isn't punished immediately. It is important not to psychoanalyze these two divergent camps or to make judgments about which group is right. These people represent the depth of the congregation's trauma. For every outspoken critic or supporter, others feel so deeply hurt that they can't sort or express their feelings.
>
> The small congregation needs to realize that this misconduct did not happen to them because something is wrong with the church. Congregations often wonder if the offending clergy was sent to them because they are small and unimportant. The people will blame both the denomination and God for letting this happen. Further, the people will wonder whether the church can survive the incident.
>
> The effects of the abuse or misconduct will linger long after the offending clergy is removed from office. The congregation will need a long period of healing. This is where a trained interim minister is indispensable. If another pastor is simply brought in to the situation, this person will face an impossible job of recovering the congregation's trust while at the same time establishing their own ministry. Interim clergy, because they are short term and engaged for the specific task of bringing healing, are free to listen to and affirm both sides in the issue. They help the congregation through a process that re-establishes faith in the clergy, the denomination, and God.

Each of these forms of pilot error involves a crisis that threatens the church. Whether it turns out that the pastor was unsuited for ministry, incompetent, burned out, or led by a personal character defect to commit an indiscretion, dealing with the particular pastor is only the tip of the iceberg. There are greater issues involving restoration of the church's self esteem and their willingness to trust the next pastor. Surprisingly, some pastors take great glee in uncovering their predecessor's errors. Instead of engaging in the self-serving practice of making comparisons, they need to focus on healing the congregation's sense of hurt. They need to listen to people talk and then to affirm each person's feelings. The congregation may need a long time to come to the place where they can view what felt like a mid-air collision as a part of God's greater plan for their congregation.

Stormy Weather

Conflict is often mentioned as the cause of a church's decline and eventual closure. When hostilities break out in a small church, people feel uncomfortable for good reason. People join and become committed to smaller congregations because of their loving relationships and intimate expression of faith. The value of acceptance, which is often expressed by people saying about the church, "we are all like family here," is the winsome mark of small fellowships. To have an unloving small church sounds like an oxymoron. Yet even airlines that work the sunny Caribbean will encounter stormy weather. Wise flight plans note the presence of hurricanes, which threaten the safety of the trip, and map alternate routes. It is the nature of air to be windy, turbulent, and to generate storms. To enjoy the benefits of flight, we have to take this into account and learn the best approach to various weather conditions. It is the nature of human beings (even the sanctified and holy kind) to have their relationships disturbed by conflict, miscommunication, and even ill-will.

When weather is a factor in an airplane crash, the general practice of investigators is to place the primary blame on the pilot because he or she could have chosen not to fly in those conditions. One pilot of small aircraft put it this way, "... weather related crashes are considered to be caused by pilot error. The reason? The problem of weather has a simple solution. Don't fly in bad weather! As for me, I've had to scrub many of my flights due to bad weather... It is plain and simple—if you cross mother nature, she'll kill you, and it doesn't matter what your airplane is capable of."[4] If this same logic is applied to the church, then much of the responsibility for disastrous conflict in the church falls to the pastor. As a pastor, I would like to argue otherwise, but I cannot. It is not that pastors cause or control conflict. Pastors bear the immediate responsibility for adapting to conflict. One job skill is to know how to manage conflict—when to wade into it and when to fly safely around it. Pastors need to allot sufficient time in their monthly routine to understand where and why storms are brewing in the church. I have often noted how calm and assuring the voice of the airline pilot sounds, when they switch on the "fasten seat belt sign," and apologetically explain that air turbulence will make things a little rough for a while.

The modern airline pilot also has the advantage of having studied a weather map, which has given him or her an overview. They know that the presence of a storm in their path is not the mysterious vengeance of the gods, but rather the predictable outcome of weather patterns. It is hard, especially for younger pastors, to bring to a congregation the perspective needed to weather the storms of conflict. When we turn to the scriptures, it is important to note not just the winners and losers of the conflicts, which mark nearly every chapter, but also the very commonness of conflict among people of mature faith. Luke gives us a wonderful example of this in his telling of the argument that led to the separation of Paul and Barnabas (Acts 15:36-40). The "sharp disagreement" may have been painful for the participants and confusing to the new Christians at Antioch who observed this early church fight, but its net effect was that two teams went out in mission to share the gospel. God seems to have had a purpose in permitting this, as well as the many other conflicts described in the Bible. With a bit of Zen-like detachment, the church leaders and pastor of a healthy congregation can realize what they need to learn from each disturbance to the flow of decision-making, faith learning, and love in the small church. We are not bad people for having had disagreements; we are students being taught by the Spirit some very deep and complex lessons.

With this in mind, remember the following observations about conflict in the small church:

> The loss of a few families from the church family is not always preventable or even a bad thing. Some people cannot be happy within the context of the small congregation's intimate relationships. Some others habitually move from church to church. Still others leave, but then return when things settle down. Each of these provide far less support for the congregation's financial and spiritual needs than what people have been led to think. The congregation may even allow itself to express a sigh of thanksgiving once these dissenters leave.

> Avoid triangulation (acting as a go-between, shuffling messages between two opposing persons or sides). This important step reduces the destructiveness of conflict. Jesus denounced the indirect and cowardly way when he presented the following guidelines for conflict:

> "If your brother sins against you, go and show him his fault, just between the two of you. If he listens to you, you have won your brother over. But if he will not listen, take one or two others along, so that every matter may be established by the testimony of two or three witnesses. If he refuses to listen to them, tell it to the church; and if he refuses to listen even to the church, treat him as you would a pagan or a tax collector." (Matthew 18:15-17 NIV)

> People disagree because they care deeply about things. Some conflict is healthy because it consolidates energy and enthusiasm around vital

issues. The closer a controversy is to the core purpose of a church, the more important that sufficient time and opportunity for expression be provided. Congregations become stagnant when good controversy is squashed or disguised in an attempt to save everybody's feelings.

Communication can often be improved and conflicts resolved by encouraging opposing parties to understand the other's point of view. One such method is to hold a congregational meeting in which all possible solutions are listed on a board. People are then randomly placed into small groups, one group for each possible solution. Each group must come up with a defense for and a listing of possible drawbacks for that solution. When people return to the main group, there is an amazing amount of learning that occurs as each group stands to present the ramifications of an idea that they might not have before given serious consideration.

Three or four alternatives are better than two. People in a loving fellowship do not like polarization. If a controversy forces the congregation to divide into one of two camps, people will feel an urge to bail out, either by refusing to decide or by making a firm decision and refusing to budge. Those wise church leaders, who manage conflict, constantly have to promote creative compromise and alternative thinking to head off polarization.

Don't let the roosters rule the roost. In some churches, one family whose financial state enables them to claim more power than other members. In other churches a person or family may exert an unusual amount of power because the church is the one arena of life in which the person has the opportunity to dominate. These people may have psychological needs that are met at the expense of the congregation's health. The church leadership needs to take a loving attitude towards these people and say, "We care about you as an individual too much to let your money or power bribe our actions. The decision-making process of the church needs constant improvement. Our goal is to give even the smallest voices of the congregation their rightful place." It is more Christian for a congregation to make decisions according to a process that gives power to the weak than it is for them to make decisions that the powerful and wealthy consider to be wise (Matthew 5:3-16).

As the airplane pilot studies the weather map, she or he tries to predict the extent and danger of serious weather. There are times when the pilot has insufficient information to know which route is likely to leave his passengers with a queasy stomach. The pilot is not free to shift the final destination of the flight because she or he enjoys smooth flying. Just as an airline is committed to the task of delivering people as promised, so also the small church is committed to the task of making disciples in its context. Discipleship formation is not always a comfortable experience for those in the pew. Finding our congregation's unique voice for witness and social service is not a task that can be done without controversy. Those who post "no smoking" signs in the fellowship room will come into conflict with those who have invited the AA group to meet in the church. Those who want to see dollars spent on mission will lock horns with those who are concerned about the bank account. Church leaders need to realize that their discomfort on the journey is connected to their commitment to the destination. We cannot make disciples without facing stormy weather, James tells us;

> "Consider it pure joy, my brothers, whenever you face trials of many kinds, because you know that the testing of your faith develops perseverance. Perseverance must finish its work so that you may be mature and complete, not lacking anything." (James 1:2-4 NIV)

Idiot Lights

As we drive down the highway of life, isn't ignorance bliss? Suddenly a light begins to flash upon our dash board. The wording on the light may say something simple like, "oil." Or it may have a more enigmatic message like, "check engine." So you look. Yes, the engine is still there, and so is the light. Do you continue to drive or do you call for a tow truck? *Will it wait "til after tomorrow's important job interview? Can I trust it not to strand me in a tunnel on the parkway during rush hour?* We call them idiot lights for a reason. Only an idiot would ignore them. Yet most of us have done that. Each section in this chapter presents one of the idiot lights on the dashboard of small church life. They form a checklist of factors that if ignored will lead to the death of a congregation.

Low fuel—A congregation cannot survive without spiritual passion.

Being Lost—A church separated from its purpose of making disciples is going nowhere fast.

Structural Problems—The need for constant review and the courage to make decisions about structures keeps the congregation's ministries functioning smoothly.

Pilot Error—When mistakes are made, the congregation needs to seek help.

Bad Weather—It is important to know the difference between healthy and dysfunctional conflict and to act appropriately.

Small churches, because they are change-resistant organizations, tend to ignore their idiot lights. A congregation can feel perfectly good about themselves and yet, be running out of fuel, lost, or leaving unconsidered their need for significant structural change. Clergy misconduct and congregational conflicts can also be mediated or prevented by the preventive maintenance.

This chapter contains both good news and bad news. The bad news is that there is not one simple cause of church closures. No magic cure sits on the horizon to prevent thousands of small churches from ceasing to exist in the next two decades. The good news is that we can take specific and practical steps to address each of these problems. Finding a cure is not the problem—implementation is.

With the exception of the most extreme cases, every small church is capable of change. It is in analyzing and prayerfully considering our faults that we open ourselves up to God's transforming acts. Our churches are in much the same place as Nicodemus was when Jesus spoke to him about how he must be born again. Our collective lips respond in surprise, "How can this be? Are we, a fifty- or a hundred-year-old congregation, meant to adapt ourselves once again to the new circumstances we find ourselves in today?" But, Jesus does not back down from insisting that we, like Nicodemus, must be born anew (John 3:3-10).

Effective small church leadership and how it relates to the re-formation of a congregation from a group of spectators to a team and the transitional process of rebirth as it relates to the current needs of small churches are two concepts that will be important to any church leader who wishes to implement a lasting solution to the idiot lights they see blinking on their dashboard.

1 *Planting New Churches in a Postmodern Age* by Ed Stetzer (Nashville: Broadman & Holman, 2003), p. 10.

2 *Faith Communities Today: A Report on Religion in the United States*, a statistical study and narrative sponsored by the Hartford Institute for Religious Research, Carl S. Dudley and David Roozen (March, 2001, available at hartsem.edu) p. 26.

3 *Julius Caesar*, Act III, scene 2

4 Paul Gray on his website flyinglightplanes.tripod.com

Chapter Five

Lead, Follow, and/or Get Out of the Way

Imagine that I take an unopened soda can and shake it and then place it on a table. The instant I pull the tab, a fountain of foam will erupt from the can. But as long as I do not open it, there will be no evidence of bubbles. In fact if we were to X-ray the can, one would see very few bubbles. In a similar fashion, examine an unopened bottle of champagne (or sparkling grape juice if you prefer) for bubbles. Pop the cork and the pent-up energy of the gas becomes evident. Released from its constraint, the wine foams over, and even when poured in an open glass, it contains an effervescence that continues for a long time. Obviously, the bubbles need room to form and display their latent energy. People, in a similar fashion, need permission to display their capacity for service in God's kingdom.

Peter Marshall wrote, "Church members in too many cases are like deep sea divers, encased in suits designed for many fathoms deep, marching bravely to pull out plugs in bath tubs."[1] Marshall wrote this in the post-war period when biblical literacy and the formal training of laity was much higher in this country than it is now. Today it would be more apt to say that our membership are like deep sea divers who believe that they can't pull out a bath tub stopper because they lack the years of theological education needed to use the Bible.

While this observation applies to any sized church, the small church lives too close to the margin to permit this kind of foolishness. If we define the small church as a congregation that survives and thrives with a model for ministry that is different than the "normal" one church–one clergy model, then small church vitality depends upon equipping and employing the laity. In the small church, each person who attends brings important and often indispensable talents and spiritual gifts. These, however, remain hidden until they are given room to bubble up.

Given the appropriate setting, support, and training, every person has the desire and capacity to act as a leader. We saw this in our children when they were very young; as long as a parent was present, their first instinct was to look to the adult for guidance. When they played in a separate room, the oldest would take charge. We would remark that our daughter was much more of a follower than a leader. But when she found herself among her peers, and felt comfortable that the setting was just right for her own unique input, she would show herself to be a leader in remarkable ways.

Our culture has so bought into the heroic myth of the great leader that we are blind to how dependent upon context leadership actually is. Given the right context, leaders form like bubbles in a glass. In the right context fellowship groups coalesce into teams with each member freely offering for the common good their own talents and personal witness to faith while also recognizing their own limitations and depending upon another in the group to cover their weakness. The right leader for these teams is often someone who would not exhibit leadership outside the trust they have come to know within the group they are leading. Leadership is shared among the different members or exercised in such a way as to give credit for accomplishments to the group rather than to the leader. This is a critical understanding for the small membership church because, in the fellowship of a few families meeting each week for worship, there exists an intimate context for the Holy Spirit to powerfully work that elevates formerly unrecognized people into leadership. This effervescence of the Spirit is like the bubbles rising to the surface of champagne (see Matthew 9:17). As the apostle Paul says it:

> ...those parts of the body that seem to be weaker are indispensable, and the parts that we think are less honorable we treat with special honor. And the parts that are unpresentable are treated with special modesty, while our presentable parts need no special treatment. But God has combined the members of the body and has given greater honor to the parts that lacked it, so that there should be no division in the body, but that its parts should have equal concern for each other.
>
> (1 Corinthians 12: 22-25 NIV)

It would be a mistake to think that Paul is simply appealing for us to be nice to those who are shy or less talented in our midst. This passage is in the context of Paul's greater vision of the church as a body where every member brings to the whole an indispensable gifted-ness. The Holy Spirit works within the hearts and lives of every individual Christian, so that each is equipped to contribute to the church exactly what that team needs to fulfill its purpose of making disciples and witnessing to Christ. The leaders oversee and guide the process of lay empowerment, ensuring that the church is a healthy team system, producing leaders and accomplishing goals. This requires those who take on the mantle of clergy to both lead and follow and to be intentional about choosing the right occasions to get out of the way.

To be an effective leader in the small church, whether as a pastor or as a significant lay person, one needs a certain optimistic faith in the work of the Holy Spirit to raise up the people for the mission and life of that church. It is very easy for pessimism to prevail, to assume that since the number of human beings present in a small church is low, that human resources will be sparse.

The Ladder of Trust

The church is a community that has been formed for the express purpose of making disciples.[2] This process is relational. Persons entering this community are not just subjected to teachings about God; they are invited to become parts of the body, and in a relatively short period of time, to view that fellowship as one of the primary relationships of their lives. Inside this family atmosphere, the nurturing of one's faith depends upon growing deeper in love and trust for the other members of the church as well as for God.

Communities exist at different levels of intensity. Individual members and the church as a whole can choose to take their relationships up or down a notch. Dating relationships share a similar dynamic. Persons who date find as time goes on that their relationship goes through different phases and even redefines itself as they move towards a deeply committed love and possibly a marriage. The community spirit of a church can also progress to new levels and then, on occasion, recede. When people lack the courage, commitment, faith, or more often, wise pastoral counsel, to remain at a higher level, they fall back to a safer level of community where the landscape looks less frightening. Unfortunately, the task of sharing the gospel with one's neighborhood in today's hostile religious environment requires a high level of teamwork from a church, especially from a small church that may have self-esteem issues to overcome.

I picture the levels of community as a ladder, which, for this discussion, has three rungs. {figure 5.1--the ladder of community)

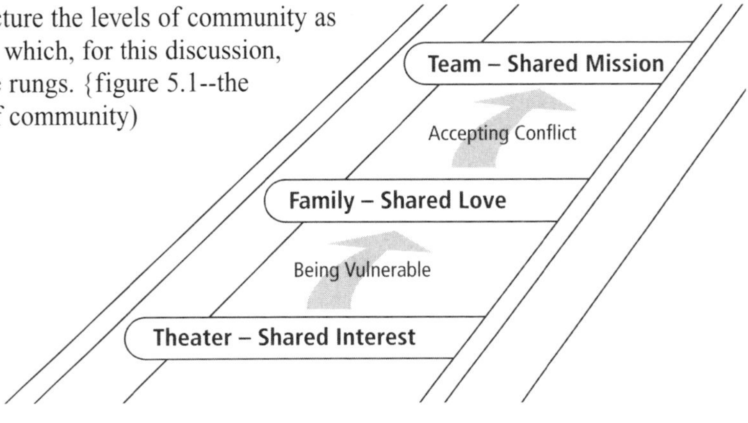

I call the first rung of the ladder the community of the Theater because each participant is either a spectator or an actor, such as the pastor who comes from the outside to perform. The community interactions are just barely above the level of civility demonstrated by strangers on the street. People gathering at a movie theater or attending a sports event have this degree of community.

They sit together and experience the same presentation. They may laugh, cry, or applaud together, but they lack any interdependence other than the warmth of shared expression. Many churches remain near to this bottom level of community, which lacks the intensity necessary for discipleship formation. When people are not vulnerable with each other, they converse about issues with uninvolved, objective language. The people may publicly display affection for each other, but when they ask, "How are you doing?" it is a rhetorical question. They are unlikely to phone or visit with each other outside of church. It is a community formed by shared interest, physical proximity, and social pleasantries, but not spirit. They may have a gifted pastor or music leader who helps to provide an excellent worship experience, but they are not engaged in the more difficult task of forming a nurturing faith Family (Rung Two) or becoming a Team, the third rung of the ladder. Without vulnerability, the church cannot go beyond simply meeting around a shared set of interests such as worship and the occasional educational program. A church on the first rung of community has limited its commitment to what feels safe, which usually involves sitting and waiting for someone from the outside to deliver the goods. They are consumers, and those pastors who serve them often feel drained by the exertion of meeting these consumer needs.

The movement off this first rung always involves vulnerability. No simple trick or boxed program is available to lead a community of people to become more vulnerable with one another. Progress in community building is almost always led by a few committed lay people who intuitively grasp the need for community, and together with the pastor set about encouraging deeper relationships. They must persistently reward and recognize situations where risk has been taken. Sometimes an event, such as working together to recover from a flood or tornado or to act in support of a neighborhood need, will become an experiential moment for leading people into deeper community. It is not simply a matter of teaching about love; instead, the interpersonal relationships must be enhanced through interventions by leaders who intentionally build trust. Everything that Jesus taught can be presented in a two-day seminar, but Jesus intentionally walked his disciples through a three-year experience. Why? It took at least that long to raise them to the level of effective community that the early church needed to do its work after Jesus' ascension.

One way to develop this vulnerability is to set aside specific time for personal sharing in the context of Bible studies and committee meetings. A sensitive leader will note the shifts between objective and subjective language in the course of a discussion and gently encourage the group to be more vulnerable with one another. Most small churches engage in chit-chat or small talk at the start of meetings. Pastors and other leaders may be inclined to corral the group and move on with the agenda. If the group leader does not check this impulse, they may do great harm. Long-time members of the small church have grown over the years to trust one another, and the pre-meeting chit-chat reaffirms this trust. They check in with each other on a personal level and practice the subjective language they will use during the meeting. During this time, each person reveals something of him or herself before the group moves on to do the more tangible business. Remember that the ultimate agenda of the church is disciple-making, and that cannot be accomplished without intentional community building.

Small church pastors need to confront their own reluctance about vulnerability. It is easy to hide behind one's authority as a minister and not enter into the community building. In this important dimension of church life one leads by example, and to foster deeper levels of trust between members of the congregation, the pastor must reveal the weaknesses of his or her own soul. Pastors need to see honesty and transparency as tools of the trade, perhaps not with the congregation as a whole, but at least with the leadership core of the church. If the pastor's hidden agenda is to use this small church experience as a stepping stone towards something bigger, then that fact will become soon revealed in intimate communities. None of the pastor's other gifts for ministry will have much effect or be appreciated because the primary task of helping the congregation progress to the highest rung of community formation will be left undone.

The second rung, by contrast, is the community of a Family. Here there is shared love and active interaction on a personal level. Like a healthy family, there is a frequently stated respect for each individual's contribution to the forward progress of the community. The church also tolerates those whose behavior frustrates the forward momentum of the church. Having conquered their fears about vulnerability, the members now devote their energies toward maintaining a culture of mutual acceptance. This aspect of community makes the small church decision-making process so consensus oriented.

In a church that has moved to this rung, people regularly share their feelings, experiences, personal histories, and faith journeys. They socialize outside the church and take seriously the need to pray for each other. Because members are now framing the issues in the context of their own experience, they are vulnerable to the group rejecting not just this insight, but also the person who offers it.

One pastor tells of moving to a highly dysfunctional small church. A former leader had pushed through many projects and improvements to the church facility. When the congregation lacked the energy and resources to keep up with him, this leader paid for the projects out of pocket and made things happen on his own. No longer able to trust that their reservations or concerns would be heard, the other members of the congregation receded down to the first rung of the community ladder. This polite acquiescence frustrated the leader until he sparked a conflict and left. The new pastor wisely spent time rebuilding community. As time went by, she was amazed by how much discussion the smallest change evoked. The chair of trustees did not buy the paint for the new front door until every member had been given a chance to put in their two cents about the color. Consensus building was becoming a shared value of the congregation and a essential part of the way they experienced community.

This rung, however, is not the final resting place of a congregation. A community that has become like a family has the capacity to nurture its own internal discipleship, but often remains too inwardly focused to impact the neighborhood. Assimilation of new members becomes a problem for the small church on this rung. Larger churches overcome this problem by constantly forming new groups, so that newcomers can come in on the bottom rung of newly-formed communities. In the small church it becomes the duty of certain doorkeepers to look and care for newcomers and intentionally introduce them to the history and customs of the congregation. Like Barnabas taking Paul by the hand and introducing him to the early church, these people inform the newcomer that unconditional acceptance really is a part of the congregation's lifestyle and values (Acts 9:26-27).

The next rung, identified as Team, calls the congregation to sacrifice some of its consensus orientation in order to become more task oriented. In sports, the players must move beyond simply accepting one another's strengths and weaknesses; they also hold one another accountable for results. They speak up when they think the actions of another team member are jeopardizing the team--in this example, the capacity of the church to make disciples for Christ. The leaders have to risk some of the security of the family-oriented community to become what Christ calls the church to be. This requires the expression of critical thought and spiritual discernment as each person brings impressions of how the church is progressing towards its goals.

To understand the need to move towards the next stage of community, the congregation has to become reacquainted with God's love for the world. The top rung of the ladder moves people beyond the church walls. It is a frightening vantage point, and most small churches will advance and retreat many times before fully committing to this step. This top rung is marked by a willingness to be called into account for results. It places such a high value on what the team accomplishes together that the personal egos of the individual members are pushed to the background.

I have most intensely experienced this team level of community among actors in a Christian theater production and not in the church. Gifted actors were willing to assume lesser roles in order to make the play come to life. Everyone pitched in together to search for appropriate props and to redesign sets and costumes even when it meant staying late into the night. Because the play was the thing, the team had an external goal to band together. There was also a willingness to speak critically of one another and to hold one another to task for forgotten lines and missed cues. The love experienced at the team level of community is not held together by mutual acceptance (as was the second rung), but rather by a shared interest in results.

Jesus' words need careful attention at this point:

> "Do you think I came to bring peace on earth? No, I tell you, but division. From now on there will be five in one family divided against each other, three against two and two against three."
>
> (Luke 12:51-52)

To move from the second to the third rung of the ladder requires the members of the congregation to accept the special role that reasonable conflict plays in team building. Conflict can be hurtful and destructive in a small church, but the fear of conflict can lock a group into protecting one another's feelings rather than accomplishing a task. The team-centered community, however, learns how to not be paralyzed by the need to keep everyone happy. This is a big step. If I do not fully trust a group, it feels safer to accept that what everyone says is of equal validity. But if I not only trust the group, but also realize that the group all shares a common interest in reaching a goal, then I can risk disagreeing with how some of the group members wish to go about reaching that task. I can say, "You're wrong about this or that," without attacking another person because we share a group relationship and a common goal. At this stage of community, what the members individually care about is evaluated by the group. Instead of working to smooth differences, the process shifts towards frank discussion and, sometimes, disagreement. The leaders now work to guide the decision-making process so that the group, after discussing all options, makes a decision. How they make the decision does not matter as much as the team's decision. For them community is no longer dependent upon consensus nor is it constrained to do only those things that offend no one. The members have become trusting enough of the process to support whatever the team chooses to do.

A typical conflict may follow this line: Bob says, "I hear the Boy Scouts would like to meet in our basement and I think that this would be a great thing for our witness as a church."

Sally responds, "We just replaced the carpet downstairs so that we could make our fellowship time more appealing to newcomers. I would hate to see the boys mess it up."

In this situation the conflict cannot be negotiated to a middle ground. As Sally and Bob presented their arguments, they appreciated that the other person's opinion was based upon the mutually held goal of witnessing to the neighborhood. Bob and Sally appreciate each other as needed members of the team, even though they differ on this issue. When the vote was finally taken, the loser supported the winner in carrying out the group's decision. The group leader ensured that both Sally and Bob fully stated their opinion and that the group did not sidestep the issue by suggesting an unworkable compromise. The group's conviction that the church needs to reach out to the community held the team together.

While this three-rung ladder of community formation exists in larger churches and even in secular organizations, it is most easily seen in the small church. In churches with more than seventy-five in attendance, the question, "What type of community shall we be?" needs to be purposefully answered by each small group within the church. A group that gets together for a senior's lunch or bowling does not need to progress beyond the first rung of the community ladder. A mission team going from the church to do service work or a youth group or a covenant-based Bible study group may agree together that the highest level of community is worth achieving. The church that wants to serve the Lord should seriously consider how building a team relationship in their church council will energize their ministry.

I think that a small church of less than seventy-five in attendance is by definition a small group, called into existence to be community of believers. To have the energy to effectively make disciples, the small church must have the courage and persistence to reach for the highest rung of the community ladder. The small church that remains in Theater mode will feel cold and reserved. A small church on the Family rung will feel warm and friendly, but they have placed limits, both on what they are willing to share with each other, and on what they are willing to achieve for Christ. The few small churches that strive to become effective Teams for Christ's service, however, have an almost electric presence to them. They are constantly making a buzz in their neighborhood by the audacity of what they commit themselves to do. They carry the task of disciple making far beyond their walls.

What grows between each rung of this ladder is the spirit of trust in the congregation. This use of *trust* needs clarification. Normally we say that we trust someone or an organization when we have concluded that their behavior is predictable and unlikely to cause us harm. The use here of the word *trust* is a statement about our level of confidence in the other person or group. When *trust* is used to describe the quality of a congregation working to become a team, it relates to the interdependence, shared goals, and intensity of relationships among the members of the community. One cannot speak about trust without acting in ways that increases one's vulnerability and stimulates productive conflict.[3]

This trust enables pastors to be effective in their role, no longer working to keep a lid on things, but rather rejoicing to see the laity uncorked and the church discovering its mission. This trust enables laity to be vulnerable with one another and with their pastor, asking for help when the tasks of ministry overwhelm them and offering support freely to those in need. Another word for this trust is the more excellent way of love, which Paul described:

> Love is patient, love is kind. It does not envy, it does not boast, it is not proud. It is not rude, it is not self seeking, it is not easily angered, it keeps no record of wrongs. Love does not delight in evil but rejoices with the truth. It always protects, always trusts, always hopes, always perseveres. Love never fails.
>
> (1 Corinthians 13:4-8 NIV)

Representative Democracy

There are two models for clergy-lay relationships in the church. The most common, and the one which is universally considered to be 'normal," can be pictured this way. {Figure 5.2}

In this model the clergy come to the local church as a representative of the denomination. The clergyperson will feel a sense of obligation to enforce the denomination's standards and rules within the local church. Often he or she will be the only person in the congregation who is aware of the legislation passed at the last denominational assembly. She or he is the lone voice telling the local church leaders that "our rules require the Trustees to be one-third women," or "on the next Sunday we will take a special offering to support the denomination's college fund." This role of lone representative is frustrating and counterproductive to the process of building a strong congregational team.

An inherent tension persists in this model, especially in those areas of church life where the clergy and laity do not feel free to share openly with one another. The laity know that their pastor will be secretive about plans to move to another situation and about the circumstances that caused the pastor to leave the last church. If clergy turnover is frequent, the congregation will develop its own protective secrets, sometimes hiding bank accounts or shutting the pastor out of the discussion of certain issues. Relatively early in my ministry, I was appointed to a five-church parish. For two decades this parish had received, on average, a new ordained pastor every three years. Meanwhile, a nearby part-time lay pastor had acted as associate to each of these transient, and often young, senior pastors. The churches viewed the lay associate as their real pastor, and they received the leadership of their lead minister with a grain of salt. Often during council discussions, the people would wait for the associate's opinion before they cast their own votes. There was little the long time lay pastor could do to shift the people's habit of deferring to him nor could he make people feel respect for the transient senior clergy. The parish offered little incentive for an ambitious and highly trained ordained pastor to remain long there. In this case, the intuitively developed roles assigned by the congregation were in direct conflict with the hierarchically assigned roles mandated by the denomination.

Every small membership church will experience tension between its values and the hierarchical framework of the denomination. Small church values mean that these congregations tend to be locally minded and place a high value on context-sensitive, "we have our own way" solutions to problems. Even when they feel good about their denomination, the small church laity tend to think of it as a clergy union or as a fraternity of spiritual wizards. They find the political machinery of the denominational office incomprehensible and suspicious with its secrets and power to wreak harm on the little church. Often the clergy representative becomes the lighting rod for congregation's resistance to the changes promoted by the denomination. The fact that the local church usually has a lay representative go to the denominational gathering does little to defuse the concerns that someone far away has the power to decide things that contradict "the way we've always done things here."

Moving to the bottom of the model, the congregation elects its representatives to the various local church offices. The advantage of this yearly ritual is that it separates those who have been made to feel guilty enough to take an office from those who plan not to do anything this year but show up and put something in the plate. The small congregation rightfully feels uncomfortable with any process that sets some people over the congregation as a whole. I am amazed at how willing volunteers are to do what needs to be done in the small church, provided I didn't organize it according to some hierarchical structure. In the small church equality is more important than organizational clarity. By the same token, because very few small churches have gone beyond the second rung of the community formation process described above, their decision-making process leans more toward consensus rather than taking votes with winners and losers. This connects with the small church's high value on enduring relationships. They would rather continue something which does not suit, but on which all can agree rather than to push through a decision which offends a long-time member.

There is a hope that clergy and lay leadership will learn to work together. The congregation may or may not choose its representatives with an eye to finding people who will work well with the pastor. If they are distrustful of the process, they may surface leaders who have a gift for confrontation. The denominational leadership usually tries to send a pastor they think will "play nice" with the local church leaders and bridge this tension. On occasion, however, the denominational leadership may send someone with the task of "putting the congregation in line." It is rare that a healthier congregation emerges from this confrontation unless the minister is an intentional interim. A well-trained interim minister knows that the task is not to make the church conform to the denomination's expectations, but to bring about healing. Interim pastors will establish a process that restores trust on both sides while introducing new options and ways of communicating. They will also take the heat for removing from office the local lay leadership who are unable to accept change. The intentional interim minister uses the brief time in the parish to provide the congregation and the new pastor a fresh place to begin.

In this model, there is a meeting place between the clergy, who is the representative of the denomination, and the local church leaders, who are the representatives of the laity. Both sides come to this meeting place in order to accomplish the work of the church. A number of tasks or functions need to be addressed. There needs to be preaching (P), worship leadership (WL), musical direction (M), pastoral care of the shut-in and hospitalized (PC), oversight of finances (F), and care for the building (B). People perform many other tasks and roles. Some may be temporary and unique to this congregation. Other tasks may be done silently by people who simply do this particular work. Their efforts may go unnoticed until the day they make a mistake or fail to do the job. The elected structure of small church officers rarely reflects the actual way things are getting done. The church rule book may include standard guidelines. Each congregation, however, develops a rich tradition that goes beyond the letter of the law. The smaller the congregation, the more unique and divergent from standard practice is the day-to-day ritual for accomplishing church.

Each task, whether it be preaching (P) or caring for the building (B), needs to be shared between the representative of the denomination and the representatives of the people. There is, as mentioned before, an inherent tension to the system. The clergy, because they are trained and professional and representing the denomination, do not want to give away a task to a lay person who may drop the ball. *What if I go on vacation, and while I am gone the lay speaker preaches something which is untrue? What if a Sunday school teacher, who lacks my theological credentials, does something silly like offer to baptize the favorite dolls of the children?* And yet the pastor, especially the small church pastor who may be serving a circuit, cannot be everywhere and do everything. Some pastors compensate for this dilemma by pretending to be all-knowing and omnipresent. They may become angry when something happens in the church that they don't know about or cannot control. The laity have a similar dilemma. They pay a lot of money for their clergy, so they want to get a lot of work from him or her. But they don't know if they can trust their pastor to take over something, because she might change things. For the lay leadership, the best solution is the one practiced by mushroom farmers; they keep their pastor in the dark and feed them lots of compliments.

There is a more serious problem to this adversarial division of labor. The Holy Spirit gifts each believer with the abilities the church needs to fulfill its task, provided all work together in humility and respect for each other. Church leadership has a bubble-up quality. The lay person can only find joy and fulfillment in Christian service if they receive room to act out of their spiritual giftedness. This latent energy becomes an irresistible force for the people of any small church engaged in discipleship formation. This force may encounters an immovable object in the form of a pastor who is concerned that he or she do what they are expected to do. *If I let a lay person preach, and I am not on vacation, what message does that send to my church treasurer who writes my paycheck?* Some pastors, especially new ones, are concerned that they may succeed in empowering the laity and then have things happen out of the pastor's control in the church, causing the denominational home office to question their effectiveness in ministry.

Three things allow this model to function despite its tension and contrary forces. First, pastors do come, in a short period of time, to love their congregations and to want what is best for the church. The loving pastor becomes involved in the serious work of empowering the laity. Second, congregations do come to trust their pastor. Provided the pastor doesn't refer to the denomination too often or push for too much change that contradicts local wisdom, they will develop a loving, working relationship together. Third, both pastor and laity fall back on some shared role expectations regarding who does what. The pastor accepts that he or she will prepare and preach a sermon almost every week. The laity accept the role they have in maintaining the church building. These roles are not written in the rulebook, but are developed by tradition, with an eye to what works. These roles become part of the oral tradition, which needs to be imparted at the beginning of each new pastor's ministry. Here too, my experience has been that the smaller the congregation, the more these roles diverge from anything taught in seminary or dreamed of in the denominational home office.

Each time a new pastor arrives in a parish, the expected roles for clergy and lay come into a new state of disequilibrium. Most congregations assume that the way they have divided the tasks between clergy and lay makes sense and will work equally well for each pastor. The clergy arrive with the idea that what worked in the last situation will work here. Each party is poised for miscommunication and conflict over roles. The new pastor will fail to meet all expectations and seem too lazy, by some standards, to do the things that "everyone knows are a pastor's job." The pastor will inadvertently step on someone's toes by doing tasks which a lay person is currently doing well. The clergy soon find themselves scrambling to do tasks that they weren't aware were their job while also trying to find out why people are angry when he or she does pastoral tasks developed in another community. It may take many years to reconcile this role confusion. In the meanwhile, the new pastor has become too busy and confused to set about the task he or she was sent to do; that is, empower the laity.

The current standard model, with its emphasis on the clergyperson as the representative of the denomination and the active lay leadership being the elected representatives of the people, contributes to this role confusion by fostering the assumption that clergy and laity have separate roles. In small churches where clergy turnover is high and denominational trust is low, little good can be said for the current model.

A Better Way

I am not entirely convinced that Jesus meant the work of the church and the roles of its leadership to be so clearly segregated into clergy and lay responsibilities. He never once listed a separate set of duties or tasks for those who would professionally follow him. In fact, Jesus seems to be concerned that the Christian movement might become as hierarchical as Temple worship had become in his day. He did not want to see the work of disciple-making get divided between the things religious professionals did and the tasks which could be trusted the ordinary people, so he gave this seldom followed command:

> "But you are not to be called 'Rabbi,' for you have only one Master and you are all brothers. And do not call anyone on earth 'father,' for you have one Father, and he is in heaven. Nor are you to be called 'teacher,' for you have one Teacher, the Christ. The greatest among you will be your servant."
>
> (Matthew 23:8-12 NIV)

The word *ordination* does not appear in the New Testament, though Paul does list the character requirements for those who are deacons, elders, and bishops in the new church. The model of clergy representing the denomination and taking on certain tasks within the local congregation stands in stark contrast to the dynamic and organic model Paul uses when he describes the church as the body of Christ. Paul notes that the church includes various functional positions, such as apostles, teachers, prophets, and healers, but these groups will not be separated from each other. Instead, Paul writes:

"But God has combined the members of the body and has given greater honor to the parts that lacked it, so that there should be no division in the body, but that its parts should have equal concern for each other.. Now you are the body of Christ, and each one of you is a part of it."

(1 Corinthians 12:24-25, 27 NIV)

The model that more closely fits these biblical understandings is that of the local congregation as a team. Good teams have the flexibility to assign the various tasks among their members dynamically, flexing to meet new conditions. The clergy, then, come into the local church prepared to do whatever tasks are necessary, but having the specific function of being a team leader. Their chief concern is to help the congregation function better together so that the church can be about the business of doing its ministry.

Instead of being hierarchical, with the denomination hovering over the local church and trying to impose its will, the team model looks like this: {figure 5.4}

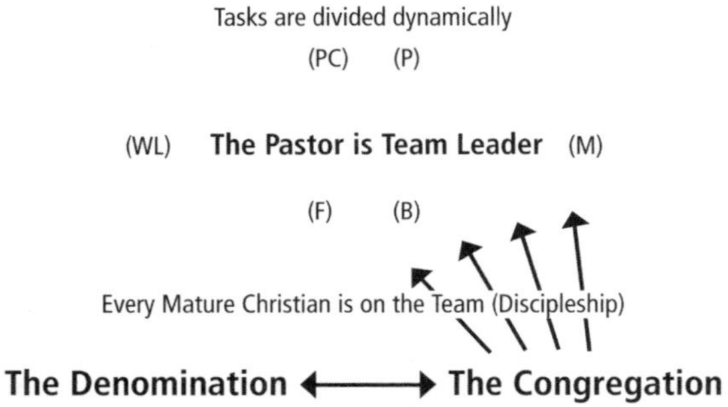

A teamwork model for doing church carries with it certain assumptions:

Clergy are not paid because they are better trained or work harder than the unpaid laity. They are paid because they coordinate the process of team building. In shared ministries, the lead pastor may actually preach less often and with less skill than lay speakers. The lead pastor will have earned his or her keep by exercising their gift of discernment in discovering and training the right people to lead worship.

Clergy will be sent to serve the small church, not because it's the bottom rung on the ladder, but because they have shown the best skills in developing teams. In the future, a major part of the clergy role in rural areas, where small churches abound, will be the development of regional shared ministries. In the inner city, clergy will work to connect congregations to the mission work going on around them. Small churches because their intimate relationships convert so easily into teams, will be on the forefront of what is exciting in ministry.

Clergy will need to become "locally minded," just as the small congregations they serve already are. Instead of being responsible for denominational standards within the local church, they will seek creative ministries within this particular context.

Clergy will need to stay put. The task of team development may require a life-long commitment to ministry in one local setting.

Laity will no longer elect a few representatives to hold down the tasks clergy let them do in the church. Instead, everyone who is mature in faith becomes a disciple of Christ. Being a disciple in Christ means being in service. Each person must discover what the gifts of the Holy Spirit within. Lay ministry will bubble up in the small church.

Laity will reconnect with the global mission of the church. Their clergy will be too busy building teams to represent denominational concerns. The laity must develop their own passion for making disciples beyond their local context. The denomination will then belong to them rather than to the clergy.

Laity must grow in the spiritual disciplines. They must read the Bible daily, trust in the power of their own prayers, and take responsibility for making the worship services more inspiring. With the advent of the internet, most everyone has equal access to quality resources. Information is no longer the exclusive province of professional guilds, such as the clergy of one's denomination.

Laity must exercise fully and freely the gifts of compassion as they minister to one another. No longer will we talk about pastoral visitation or pastoral care. Instead we will talk about how the people of the church shepherd each other and care for the weak.

The small church will no longer be a stand-alone unit. Congregations will team up with other congregations in order to do ministry to their region. Churches will not simply share a pastor as they do today. They instead will share ministry with a number of other congregations and have one or two clergy acting as team leaders facilitating the process.

Congregations will have greater freedom and responsibility to choose who they share ministry with. Many churches will exercise this freedom by crossing denominational lines and finding partners in differing traditions. Clergy, as they work to facilitate these new relationships, will forget who belongs to which denomination.

Leading with your Wallet

Many people assume the reason a small church stays small is because it lacks money. Some small church members, when asked to describe their beloved church, say, "We're just a little poor church. Nobody much wants to join us because we don't have much to offer. They all go to the big church where the rich people are." The logic is that all small churches are by necessity limited and poor. This poverty mentality assumes that God has chosen to keep this particular church poor in order to keep the people inside it humble. This form of thinking is as theologically substantial as Swiss cheese. By thinking this way, parishioners place the blame on God for the church's lack of vitality. After all, if God had wanted the church to offer more, God would have made it larger. Equally insubstantial is the opinion held by some clergy and denominational officials that smallness and the lack of financial stability are the twin punishments that God inflicts upon the unfaithful congregation. If they were more "spiritual," God would bless them with everything they need and they would grow larger.

Stewardship is a component of every church's life. When the stewardship is healthy, then additional avenues open up for the church to serve God's kingdom. The church's numerical size may or may not be effected by these additional opportunities for outreach. The importance of good stewardship to church vitality applies to all sizes of churches and should be addressed whenever the church leadership discusses the life of their congregation. Good stewardship is the product of two factors: effective leadership and spiritual passion. Spiritual passion means that people are not driven by guilt, but lead by their enthusiasm for seeing God's kingdom advanced. Effective leadership means that newcomers to a congregation see positive examples of good stewardship habits in the lay and clergy leadership of the church. They quickly adopt for themselves the giving habits and expectation of generosity they see evidenced by the people beside them in the pew. This is a further reason why just getting more people in the door rarely bails out a struggling church. But in the small church, a few people who are willing to model their own faithful stewardship to their fellow members can turn the congregation around.

In a small church, the health of the congregation's stewardship can be easily measured. Look at a list of the regular contributors and place beside each name a rough guess of their annual income. Be sure and destroy this paper afterwards! If only part of a household is faithful or favorable to the church, then list only the part of the household's income that the church attendee controls. Do not assume that retirees have a limited income. Those who retired during the 1990's often have better stock and pension benefits than those who are currently working. Consulting demographic data for your region (much of this is on the internet) may help with your estimate. It is not important that you accurately guess the income of any one contributor. The idea is to guess as many high as you guess low. Total this column and compare this figure to the annual giving received by the church. What percentage is annual giving of the total income of church contributors?

(Formula) Total Income of all Contributors / Total Yearly Giving = ? %

Tithing, or sharing one tenth of one's income with God's work, is a standard presented throughout the Bible. For reasons that go beyond the scope of this work, I and most church writers assume that a group of people who are fully committed to their fellowship, who have sufficient spiritual passion and are spiritually mature, will give about ten percent of their annual income to the fellowship. Some mature Christians divide their tithe between their church and other charities, but in most church settings, they are counterbalanced by those who give offerings to the church beyond their tithe.

By contrast, the average giving of people in our culture to charity is about two percent. This being said, two percent of the total income of their contributing families would be the bottom, minimum expectation of a church. Here the congregation behaves as if it has received no more training or Christian insight into the process of setting aside money for the needs of others than their secular, non-church attending neighbors. Two percent also marks the bottom floor of commitment a family might make to the local church leadership. People naturally shift their charitable giving toward causes whose people and goals are familiar and appear trustworthy. A drop below two percent is a warning light, indicating a lack of health in the congregation.

Ten percent would mark the ideal expectation of giving by the congregation. This level is not realistically achievable, however, because in a healthy congregation, there will always be new Christians and new attendees assimilated into the congregation's culture. These people lower the congregation's average level of giving. With this in mind, I offer the following chart:

below 2%	indication of a deeper congregational problem
2 to 4%	low congregational stewardship training
5 to 6%	moderate stewardship quality
7 to 9%	highly developed stewardship training and participation
10% or above	unusual circumstance. The congregation may not be receiving new members. There might be a controlling dogma that does not allow attendees to freely choose what they want to give.

Every congregation is a mixture of contributors. This distribution of different financial gifts has ramifications for every church, no matter the size. A church can have a number of wealthy members but suffer from limited financial resources if the majority of their givers range closer to the two percent figure. A church can be entirely made up of people of limited means, but if there is both spiritual passion and appropriate stewardship education, they will thrive and support exciting outreach beyond their walls.

If stewardship is low, education and personal leadership by example are important. People need to be taught how to give. People who are nearer to the two percent end of a congregation's giving distribution tend to give a set amount, based on convenience. This may be a dollar or two, or perhaps a ten-dollar bill, but their gift will not approach their gift if they based the gift upon a percentage of their income. New Christians and recent arrivals to a congregation will look around to discover the expectations of the fellowship. If there are active laity who express their own commitment to tithing and a generous spirit towards the special mission projects the church supports, the new attendee will accept the higher expectations as a part of the congregation's culture. It is the obligation of both the pastor and the laity to encourage each attendee to make their offering a premeditated act. Giving is not to be motivated by guilt nor should it be the product of a casual glance into the wallet to see what can be spared this morning. Every small church needs a carefully planned annual stewardship campaign. The focus of this campaign should not be the church budget. Instead, teach people how to spend time in prayer deciding what percentage of their future income they will commit to this fellowship. Having decided in advance what they have committed to bring as an offering, the church attendee is now free to give cheerfully, without compulsion or reluctance. The apostle Paul wrote:

> Each of you must give as you have made up your mind,
> not reluctantly or under compulsion, for God loves a cheerful giver.
>
> (2 Corinthians 9:7)

Many churches teach this lesson through a yearly pledge drive. Commitment cards are sent out to each contributor with the expectation that they pray and then fill in the amount they are committed to contributing in the year ahead. The cards are placed upon the altar and dedicated on Harvest or Stewardship Sunday. The total commitment made on the cards aids the church leadership in planning the following year's budget. If a budget is presented before the pledge drive, it should show two columns. The first column shows what the church will do if people continue giving at their current rate. The second column shows what additional things the church could take on if the giving improves by a certain goal amount. New opportunities, rather than rising expenses, drive spiritual passion and help people choose to support the church more consistently and joyfully.

I have noticed widespread reluctance among small membership church congregations to do a pledge drive. Some of their concerns and some suggested solutions are as follows:

We respect each other's privacy here. Provide people with the opportunity to submit an unsigned pledge card. The idea is to make a prayer commitment.

I don't know what my income will be next year. The pledge card should contain a line saying that this is only an estimate of giving. Assure people that the church will not dun them for failure to pay. There is a lesson in faith that needs to be taught throughout the stewardship campaign; that is, that what we offer to God reveals our trust in God for the future.

I'm on a fixed income. Everyone's income is in some way fixed. If you are retired, be thankful that your pension is predictable and not likely to be consumed by transportation costs or high consumer interest rates that today's young families struggle with. What we choose to give expresses our faith in God, rather than our concern about our income being less than we desire.

My spouse doesn't approve of the church. Make a pledge based upon the family income or purchases that you control. Reveal that amount to them, telling them your reasons for giving. Pledging encourages you to be honest in your communication, instead of sneaking a little bit out each week.

When I do the math based upon a percentage of my income, it seems like a lot of money. That's the point! Giving is meant to be sacrificial. Knowing the cost is part of stepping out in faith. Many congregations use a "step program" or chart, which encourages people to calculate what percentage of income their current giving is, and then step up one percentage point in the next year until you reach the place where you are tithing. This gradual approach recognizes the need many have to move gradually toward the tithe.

The quality of the church's stewardship is a composite of how well people are being assimilated and educated into the Christian lifestyle and how passionate the congregation is about spiritual things. Since giving is affected by the rise and fall of spiritual passion, many congregations notice an improvement in their finances when they elevate the practice of prayer, Scripture reading, public witness, and the inspirational quality of worship. Recognize that an educational component remains part of good stewardship. Just because a church is meeting the budget this year does not mean that it can skip the yearly stewardship campaign or stop talking about tithing. Good stewardship education also requires the laity and the clergy to be in sync, sharing their commitment to leadership by example.

Leadership Burnout

Burnout is like the weather: everyone talks about it, but we rarely do anything about it. When I offer a workshop on a topic related to burnout, turnout is large, and the question-and-answer period goes way beyond the time allotted. Over half of today's clergy complain about being burned out, often blaming factors such as:

Too much work to do

Too little support from the laity

Invasion of personal space (the parsonage is a fish bowl)

Constantly having to put out fires (conflict)

Too little time for spiritual renewal

Getting paid and/or appreciated too little

The lay leadership of the church also complain about being burned out. They name factors such as:

Too many jobs in the church

Having a job too long

Getting too little support from the pastor (no job training)

Getting too little help from other church members

Hearing too much complaining (conflict)

Too many meetings

Not receiving from worship anything to renew the spirit

Getting appreciated too little

This book cannot address all of these concerns, but three fundamental observations concern burnout:

First, burnout is not caused by doing too much. It is caused by the dysfunctional relationships and psychological coping mechanisms that motivate us by guilt. Whenever we are guilt-driven rather than spirit-led, we become burned out.

Second, burnout is always diagnosed too late. Whenever a person says they feel burned out, they are near the end of an emotional and spiritual decline, which should have been reversed earlier on. It is very hard to make burnt toast edible again.

Third, it takes much longer to recover spiritually from the effects of burnout than we are willing to permit ourselves or others. God often uses this lengthy recovery time to retool us for other areas of service.

The small church, because it is intimate and focused upon long-term relationships, should be aware of and sensitive to each of these understandings. Healthy congregations provide the kind of nurturing atmosphere where people are given the time they need to recover when they feel spiritually dry. They are more interested in building community than in maximizing the work they get out of each other. They ask each other questions like, "How are you really doing with your church job? Is it getting to be too much? How can we support you?" They check in with each other. They catch burnout before it is too late. They operate out of a theology that emphasizes the joy of working together with the spirit, rather than the responsibility of having to accomplish things on your own. They talk about grace rather than works.

However, small church leaders, both clergy and lay, are prone to feel indispensable. They speak the myth, "If I don't do it, nobody else will." In doing this they may be perpetuating co-dependent behavior they learned apart from the Christ-dependent understanding that should mark church work. Each of us to prayerfully ask ourselves, "Is this the moment God is calling me to lead, or am I to follow, or am I to get out of the way?" The bubble-up principle of church leadership, presented at the beginning of this chapter, is a profound truth. Whenever a person, no matter how well-intentioned, remains in a leadership position too long, they prevent the advancement of someone else to that task. It is true that the next person may not do it as well, but this new person may need the opportunity to move into that position for their own spiritual growth.

There is, however, an important corollary to the bubble-up principle: it is that tasks in the small church that do not have the appropriate leaders may not really need to be done. This requires a big leap of faith. *What if I step down from doing something and no one takes my place? Will the church survive if this thing is left undone? What about my own pride, if the church moves along just fine without me doing that particular job?* In the small church there are times when certain functions and programs need to lie fallow. For mid-sized and larger churches, there is a long list of required committees and activities. It would be unthinkable for a larger church to be without a youth group or a choir, but many small churches function perfectly well without having these spots being covered.

One small church with fifty in attendance had a very capable person who ran a one-room Sunday school the hour before worship. After many years, she began to feel burned out. She also experienced too many Sundays when no children showed up and she had prepared a lesson for naught. When she submitted her resignation, no one felt comfortable following her. She had, however, provided the church council time to think about the issue, something churches that are not sensitive to the issue of burnout rarely experience. The next season, the church tried a different approach to meeting the needs of their children. Church school was offered during worship, and a sign-up sheet was passed around for two volunteers to team-teach. All members were encouraged to take one or two Sundays a quarter. Some people who had never taught tried it and discovered a gift for teaching. Since two people were needed each Sunday, friends signed up together and partnerships were formed. This motivated people to pick up the curriculum and review it and, unexpectedly, brought some of the elderly teachers out of retirement. The pastor expressed some misgivings about the time change that took people out of worship, but all agreed that the experiment was useful to the church for the short term. It paid a dividend in resting the one gifted teacher and also raising awareness of the Sunday school program.

Burnout among the laity is a critical problem in most small churches, partly because congregations tend to confuse stability with security. When the same person does the same job week after week, the church experiences a sense of stability. The right person is doing the right thing, and all is right with the world. The church is stable, but it is really not very secure. What if this person is tired of the job? What if they quit or leave the church? For a church to have real security, each person needs to be appropriately established in their position and given the right amount of support. A good lay assignment process for a small church might look like this:

1) The process begins when a person is presented with the opportunity to volunteer or is approached by the lay leadership committee (nominations). At this point they need to be given the opportunity to pray and to discern if the Spirit has gifted and called them to the task. Forcing a person by guilt, rather than allowing the Spirit to prompt and lead, sets up a person for failure.

2) The person must receive the proper training and tools for the task. This is why lay empowerment is such difficult and yet, important work for pastors. They need to devote large amounts of time and one-on-one conversations to help people to understand current expectations and possible ways they might express themselves creatively in ministry.

3) The task and the person's role need to be put in context of a supportive team. People need to know who they can call upon for help. They need to know how this job relates to the other tasks people are doing. What budgeted funds can they spend? To whom are they accountable?

4) As they begin their task, they need frequent contact for support and to learn if this ministry fit their gifts and whether they feel adequately trained for this job.

5) The length of service needs discussion. Is there a term limit? Will someone check with them to ask if they want to continue doing the job? How can they keep from getting in a rut?

6) They need to begin to mentor a successor. If no job description existed when they began, are they willing to help write one? Who have they shown how to do what they do?

These steps underscore a process for giving people permission to leave their job when they are ready rather than waiting for burnout. Clergy might have a hard time appreciating the above process because they rarely feel under-trained. Clergy may have grown used to jumping into new projects without discerning the Spirit. They often wonder why the laity hesitate to take on new roles. The concept of having each church worker mentor their replacement isn't on most pastors' radar screens.

Clergy often bring their burnout with them into a new situation. Since they have not addressed the work addiction and co-dependent behaviors that stressed them out in their previous church, they should not be surprised when they begin to feel burned-out in the new congregation. However, it is easier to blame the laity of this new congregation for not supporting them than it is to examine how their approach to ministry sets them up for a repeated pattern of burnout. The three understandings mentioned above need to be taken seriously and applied directly to the clergy role:

First, we clergy are not experiencing burnout because we have been forced to do too much. We have invited burnout into our lives by leaving the expectations of our dysfunctional relationships unquestioned. We have not challenged our psychological coping mechanisms (co-dependency). We have become guilt driven, rather than Spirit led. We will bring out burnout with us wherever we go.

Second, we clergy need to stop avoiding the reality of our own burnout. The sooner we take action to reverse our lifestyle and attitude, the more likely we are to return to a state of spiritual wholeness.

Third, we clergy need to make use of the slower pace and natural emphasis on loving relationships found in the small congregation in order to find our own shalom.

Most smaller congregations have a great reservoir of resiliency. They will survive while we take the time off that we need to recover our own spirituality. We might discover that, by taking the time to do this self-care, we have created the space for laity to bubble up into new positions. It will not be time for us to return to full service until we have become wiser about when to lead, when to follow, and when to step out of the way.

1 "Pastor's Postscript" from *Mr. Jones meet the Master*, a collection of Peter Marshall sermons and prayers edited by Catherine Marshall (Fleming H. Revel Company, 1949).

2 *The Book of Discipline*, 2004, The United Methodist Church, par. 121, 122

3 See *The Five Dysfunctions of a Team* by Patrick Lencioni (Jossey-Bass/Wiley, 2002) especially pp. 195-220.

Chapter Six

Sea Squirts and Butterflies

In the ocean lives a small aquatic creature common known as the sea squirt. When sea squirts hatch they have eyes, a little tail, and an active nervous system. Looking like miniature tadpoles, they swim freely about the ocean during the first stage of their lives. But when that stage of their development is over, they stop swimming. They drift to the bottom and attach their little tail to a rock. Here they begin to vegetate. Day after day they sit, sucking in the sea water and sifting it for nutrients. Their eyes disappear, their nervous system atrophies, their stomach grows larger until they begin to look like little potatoes. From now until they die, they never swim again. They just sit there, sucking the sea water in, taking what they need, and squirting it back out. It is called retrograde development, and scientists say that the sea squirt is the only creature that does this, but maybe they don't know people very well.

This chapter concerns change and transformation in the small church. There is good news and there is bad news. The good news is that small churches can engage in substantive change, despite a value system that emphasizes stability and resistance to change in the midst of a chaotic world, Many smaller congregations have already experienced renewed vitality and health by engaging in some of the changes proposed throughout this book. Some have given up the old church building, which they loved, in order to relocate to a structure that was the right size for them. Some, after decades of neglecting their context, have recovered a relationship with their neighborhood. Some have broken the cycle of clergy dependence and reformed their leadership into a team. The people of these congregations have risked being vulnerable with each other and, not resting on the comfort of this elevated sense of community, have recovered a focus on the task of reaching their community with the Christian gospel. They have renewed their sense of spiritual passion and set themselves on their own middle way of simplicity, which is both distant from stagnation and true to their own identity as a smaller congregation. Change can be wonderful in the small church.

The bad news is that many small churches are today engaging in a downhill transformation. They are making the same kind of changes we see in the sea squirt; they are models of retrograde development. These churches have allowed their contentment in being a intimate fellowship to solidify into a palpable disinterest in joining new members. They are trading spiritual passion and inspirational worship for a lifeless idolatry of their current church building. They have backed away from the risk and vulnerability that genuine community requires. They have become gatherings of spectators, hiring a preacher to do the weekly ritual. No longer contributing to the democratic flow of ideas, they sit idly by and sift out the scant spiritual nutrients that float through our contemporary culture. The most exciting thing happening at their church is the occasional sharing of a joke found on the internet. Being the church at the cross-roads of their community has become for them a mere geographic fact; it does not stir in their hearts a critical responsibility to witness about their faith. The church is here because it has always been here. They are a people with their tail rooted to a rock, but the rock is no longer Jesus.

The thing which makes the sea squirt such a frightening image for the small church is that it shows how easily slipping into stagnation can feel natural and inevitable. Did not the Lord design the sea squirt? Perhaps this is our lot. Our religious institution is destined to die upon this corner a forgotten and forsaken little chapel. Is this inevitable? In contrast to the sea squirt, most living things take the opposite path. Each new stage in their development brings increased freedom and new responsibilities. Some, like caterpillars metamorphosing into butterflies, transform themselves into remarkable creatures of the air. They enter adulthood, not just with greater freedom and beauty, but with an understanding that they must reproduce. Like churches who know they must make disciples, butterflies enter the field intent on multiplying. Reflecting on the contrasting images of the sea squirt and the butterfly raises three critical questions for today's small church leader:

1. What causes religious organization to lock into a life cycle of birth, adulthood, decline, and death? Are congregations, like sea squirts, doomed by their nature to stagnate as they get older? What are the signposts along the way that can help to turn back the institutional aging process?

2. How can the church leadership in the small church, which is normally conservative, become bullish about responding to the changes which are happening in society?

3. When is the time to choose between the image of sea squirt or butterfly? What is the spiritual gene that drives this choice? Is today the day to begin a transition, knitting the cocoon that will protect the congregation as it changes from being caterpillar to butterfly. How can we enhance that change process for success?

The Life Cycle

Recently, a number of resources have come on the market describing the life cycle of a congregation.[1] Many of these books build on the pioneering work of James F. Hopewell in congregational analysis. Churches and other social organizations experience an almost human aging process.

When they are first organized, churches are vision-driven and full of energy. All of their activities flow out of a sense of God's purpose for their congregation. They don't simply support missions; they are the mission. During this early phase of their development, churches are often highly dependent upon a visionary pastor. Life for the toddling congregation is full of mistakes and minor setbacks, but there is something irrepressible about their spirit. These are the *"Up and Coming"* churches described in chapter 3.

As they develop, congregations enter an adolescent phase in which their energy is channeled in the development of programs. The success of some of the programs keeps their enthusiasm high, but it is now apparent that many leaders, not just one visionary leader, are needed to keep up with this growth. When a church adds more programs, activities, and people to staff these activities, that church is in this developmental phase.

Adulthood for a congregation is marked by the exchange of energy for structure. Procedures are written, budgets are fixed, and rules govern every aspect of church life. They are no longer dependent upon the day-to-day decisions made by a visionary leader. They now have a process for changing pastors and a stable relationship with their denomination. Growth slows and eventually stops as the church reaches its prime. These are happy days for many small churches who hit their stride and settle into a middle way between growth and stagnation. Many of the *"Always Small"* churches mentioned in chapter 3 have no goal except to make this phase of their existence stretch out as long as possible.

Just as in human life, midlife signals a downward turn in the process. The church's statistics slowly fall off and while they still do many things, little energy remains to start new things. As this decline continues, it begins to feel normal, and those long-time members who remember the visionary days of the church's youth begin to die. No longer purpose-driven, the leadership of the congregation now base their decisions on what keeps the membership happy. The congregation shifts to an inward focus. They may gain a few members on transfer from other similar churches, but they no longer have anyone join through profession of faith. They have become a "once upon a time" church.

Decline leads inevitably to death. The things that are cherished by the remaining members of the congregation's old age contrast starkly contrast with what was valued at the beginning. When they began, the building where the congregation met was unimportant. In their final days the congregation agonizes about what will happen to their building. In their beginning they so embodied a concern for the lost people of their neighborhood that the church was itself a mission. In their final days, anything involving mission has been stripped from the budget with the words, "we can't afford that." In the beginning nobody had a plan for organization; things were put together on the fly. There was little regard for whose committee something fell under or what the rule book said. In the end, the people will value organization above everything. Even their dissolution as a congregation will be done by the rules. The church began as a team; it will die as a set of committees. They began with a vision for the future. In the end they will care so much for the past that the congregation's last act will be to insure that something has been written about them in the denomination's history book.

Is this the story of every church? One observation in all of the life cycle literature is that it is impossible to fix an age range in terms of years for any of these periods. Humans reach adulthood, at least physically, in about 18 years, and most new church starts are fully mature and in their prime in about half that time. But there are churches like Willow Creek in Barrington, Illinois who are remarkably vision-based and energetic after thirty years. And what about death? Is there an average life span for a congregation? The math makes no sense at all if you try to factor in places like the Cathedral at Canterbury, which is rooted in the sixth century. In the United States, a worshiping congregation continues at Lovely Lane Chapel, home of the Methodist Christmas Conference in 1784. These congregations, however, remind me of the person who attempted to auction George Washington's ax on Ebay. The ax was indeed genuine, but the ax head had been replaced twice and the handle four times. The oldest churches can indeed boast about their history, but most have replaced their building three times and their congregation changes with every generation. There are no any old churches, just old church mindsets.

Life Cycle theory deals with the culture of a congregation. Some congregations have a youthful culture that values energy and vision. Others have the mature culture that values quality programs and working structures. Still other have a declining culture that values comfort and security. The building may change and the people of a congregation come and go, but the culture remains as something we each contribute to and then hand on. The aging process is like a wind that continually influences the culture to shift towards an older state of being. The current church leadership cannot change the wind, but they can choose to resist it and opt for younger values. The mature church can seek to recover its vision. The declining church can halt the procession towards death if it chooses to emphasize mission over comfort.

I think the Life Cycle theory is helpful for small church leaders who wish to understand the reasons why their congregation values the things it currently values. We each need to be aware of how the decisions we make influence the culture of the church. We do not simply hand on what we have received to the next generation. We always give it a little twist. That twist of culture can either be in the direction of youth and energy or it can be in favor of old age and decline. I will emphasize the concept of church leaders making choices in discussions about congregational change.

I do not like the fatalism that many might read into Life Cycle theory. Some of today's most popular experts have made the logical jump from the fact that 3,500 congregations go out of existence each year to the conclusion that the aging and dying of small churches is inevitable. Many who are excited about the growth of megachurches or those who are engaged in church planting advocate a form of triage. For them, congregations that are old and small should be ignored or encouraged to die. Nothing can reverse the Life Cycle, they say. Congregations in their prime should give generously to new church starts because only young churches will be around for the future.

This logic may help to raise money for a very worthy cause, but it further alienates those who are committed to small church and believe that effective leadership can bring a congregation back to its intended purpose. Far from being hopeless causes, many small churches are surviving into their second century because they have constantly adapted their ministry to the needs of their neighborhood. The important thing to note is not their smallness, but that they are the only religious institution in operation in that area. New churches do not get planted where the environment is not perfect for them. Small churches, however, stay where they have been planted and learn how to grow old with grace.

Recognizing Decline

In the classic *A Christmas Carol*, Ebeneezer Scrooge is visited by three spirits: one with visions of the past, one showing scenes from the present, and the third pointing to the future. After traveling with the ghost of Christmas future, Scrooge asks an important question, "Are these things that I have been shown, visions of what must be, or can the future be altered?" The image of the sea squirt and the theory of the congregational Life Cycle should lead many small church leaders to ask the same question concerning their congregation. There are two problems with projections of the future in general, and with any analysis concerning how a small church needs to change in particular. First is that we are rarely scared or motivated enough to choose a different future. The second is that there are few guides which help us to understand our own process and what needs to be done to make this change happen.

I have noticed that small congregations whose state of decline is accelerating to the point where death seems inevitable tend to hesitate, sometimes for years, before making an appropriate response. For me the appropriate response is to choose to enter into a transitional process, which I will outline later in the section titled "The Rules of Transition." But in that period of hesitation, congregations engage in various time consuming irrational behaviors which are reminiscent of Dr. Elisabeth Kubler-Ross's five stages of grief:[2]

Denial: Churches in decline often stop keeping statistics. The fact that there are less people in worship today than a year ago is a forbidden topic. The pastor or some other church leader may try to raise the topic at meetings, but no one wants to discuss that the church is starting to die. Pastors often choose to join the denial game and work with the rest of the congregation to squelch any negative talk about the church's financial health or inability to attract new members.

Anger: When denial can no longer be sustained, the next step is to get angry at someone. It may be the pastor or the denomination or the growing church down the street. Even a good internal church fight can defer the congregation from confronting the fact that they are dying.

Bargaining: Anger requires energy and can only burn so long, then the church has to move to the emotional flip side, which involves making irrational bargains. The people may try many unusual things in hopes that they will get lucky again. A church that for years has failed to pay its denominational askings may suddenly pay them in full. If they are about to lose their pastor, they may enter convoluted negotiations to give them more time in their current state. Their search for a new pastor will be marked by promises that they cannot keep.

Depression: Here the congregation has run out of hope. They pretend not to care about the fact that the church may close. In actuality, they care so deeply that they can't talk about it. It is an unspeakable sadness for them.

Acceptance: After the period of hesitation is over, the congregation accepts that they will have to close unless a radical transformation happens. Now they can talk honestly and freely. The question, however, remains: do they have the energy and time to turn things around?

Change

Those who pastor small congregations through the grief stages often conclude that something is wrong with their lay leadership's ability to accept change. I suggest that we make a more careful and accurate appraisal of this problem. The people who accept the leadership positions in smaller congregations often take very seriously their perceived obligation to preserve the local church's traditions. They want to make sure that any changes proposed will not interfere with fundamental habits, such as worship, prayer, and fellowship. They are also aware of how many in the church have sought refuge from the chaotic changes that mark our modern society. These leaders reason that the less the church changes, the more comforting it can be for those whose personal lives have been burned out by change. Resistance to change is a product of the compassion they have for the church's members, particularly the elderly.

Further, many smaller congregations follow a consensus-based decision-making process that resists change until everyone agrees. Because the members value enduring relationships, they tend to be reluctant about anything that might cause someone to leave. The leaders of the small church can also, like every organization, uphold their values at the cost of being faithful to their purpose. They can believe that keeping the building as it is, carrying on certain traditions, and guarding that which previous generations entrusted to them is their sole purpose. They do not understand that these actions reflect many of the values they share with other small churches and may need to be sacrificed to act out the purpose God has for the church. Values, from time to time, need to be clarified and put in perspective, based upon how these values contribute to the church's greater purpose of making disciples.

It is important to realize that small churches are not by nature resistant to all change. Some have adapted to a major shift in music or liturgy without a complaint (try that in a mid-size or large church!). Others have accepted and prospered with pastors who did not match the stereotype of a pastor, even though this change altered the very root of their self-identity as a church. To be open to change, however, small church leaders need time to sort the ramifications of the action. They need to be led through a process that enables them to let go of some values in order to support other more important ones.

Change, however, is an essential fact of life, especially modern life. As Heraclitus remarked twenty-five centuries ago, you cannot step in the same river twice. The waters keep changing. No matter how conservative the people of a congregation may seem, they are not unaware of change. Before I, as a pastor, attempt to confront the lay leadership about their reluctance to make a change needed in the church, I have found it helpful to listen to them talk about recent changes they have made to their lives. We take a break and go around the table and each person reflects upon a decision they made which was risky or required them to step out in faith. One of them may have gone back to school for some mid-career retraining. Another may have taken up skiing or some other risky sport, even though he or she is well over fifty. Another recently returned from a trip to a foreign land. As I go around the table, I quickly discover that these people are not risk averse when it comes to their own lives. They greet change warmly when it happens to them personally and when they can see how the change supports one of their own cherished values. What is it about this particular change, which is being proposed for the church, that they find frightening? How can I re-frame the issue so that they see it as a choice which supports some aspect of congregational life which they value?

To be an advocate for change in the small church, we need to relate every choice back to our purpose for being a church. Christ calls us to make disciples in the midst of our own context. Christ calls us to be his witnesses. The leadership of the small church needs careful guidance so that they place other values, such as preserving the current building, in a subservient spot below that of making disciples for Christ. This form of reasoning defuses people's fear of change and makes it an expected part of church life. After all, the people of the church know that the world around them is changing and that this impacts the way the church invites people to discipleship. The demographics of our land are in flux. Our neighbors' needs are different from what they needed ten years ago. Our methods for sharing the good news also have to change. The church is lost if it doesn't engage in need-based evangelism. Lay people, when given the guidance and time to think about issues in this way, love the church too much to let it be lost.

The apostle Paul was being a great philosopher of change when he wrote, "...one thing I do: Forgetting what is behind and straining toward what is ahead, I press on toward the goal to win the prize for which God has called me..." (Philippians 3:13-14). Capitalizing on the opportunities he found in each changing mission field became a personal value for Paul, squeezing out the values which had previously controlled his pharisaic and conservative mindset. He writes, "To the Jews I became like a Jew, to win the Jews... To those not having the law I became like one not having the law... To the weak I became weak, to win the weak. I have become all things to all men so that by all possible means I might save some." (I Corinthians 9:20-22 NIV)

One also needs to keep in mind that the smaller congregation's resistance to change has nothing to do with size. Many small creatures handle change remarkably well. Seeds change into plants, caterpillars metamorphose into butterflies. But in the small church, what should be changed needs to be reflected on with an eye to both small church values and scriptural truth. The Bible tends to talk about change as a miracle that happens more by faith than by human planning. Every major change in the small church needs to be under girded with prayer. Perhaps because smaller congregations are in the most humble of circumstances, they know their dependence upon the Spirit.

The rural farmer can understand that Jesus is talking about change when he says:

> This is what the kingdom of God is like. A man scatters seed on the ground. Night and day, whether he sleeps or gets up, the seed sprouts and grows, though he does not know how. All by itself the soil produces grain first the stalk, then the head, then the full kernel in the head.
>
> Mark 4:26-28

Here the wheat seeds undergo a change that the rational person cannot understand. First the wheat is a seed, and then it dies to being a seed and becomes a growing plant. It produces a head of new seeds on the top of its stock, but just when it has successfully placed all of its energy into making the fruit, the farmer comes along and chops it down, separating the harvest from the original seed of wheat. Rural small church people understand that the kind of change God brings about is often sacrificial. They also know that it is mysterious and that it cannot be rushed. It must instead be fully supported by prayer and by taking the time to build consensus. What often frustrates outsiders looking at the small church is how the people refuse to be hurried into growth. They are like seeds who are unmoved by the farmer who runs up and down the rows, shouting, "Get up, get up, sprout! I want to have you harvested in time for my farm agency report!"

When change happens in the world and the church is adversely effected by it, it is important that congregation not come to think of themselves as victims of change. In adapting to the challenges around it, the church must constantly depend upon its faith. When change needs to be instituted by the congregation, faith again needs to be brought to the forefront. The guidelines for pastors and other church leaders who are seeking to institute change are:

– Less argument, more listening

– Less reasoning, more prayer

What the Future May Require

Throughout this book a number of major transitions have been proposed as possible avenues for the small church that seeks to stay vital and true to its purpose. A brief summary would include:

Relocating or drastically altering the church building to make the facility the right size for the ministry. A sanctuary that is too large for the worshiping congregation dampens the inspirational quality of the worship. Some churches have divided their sanctuary by constructing a parting wall. They then might use the new program space to house a food bank, provide an office for a social service agency, or to create a designated prayer room. Often in small rural communities, there will be two struggling congregations who are aware that paying to heat both church buildings is poor stewardship. The people in one small New England town came up with the solution of meeting in the United Methodist church in the winter and in the UCC church in the summer. They merged many programs and adopted a pattern of alternating which denomination provided the pastor each time there was a change. The initial union agreement allowed each congregation to retain their own membership roles, but also provided for ongoing dialogue towards greater unity. The important thing that needs to be kept in mind is that the financial reasons should not drive the process. If a merger is being considered, then each congregation needs to pray and engage in a visioning process until each can see clearly how the change will support their witness to the community. Unless the Holy Spirit can be discerned leading the church to greater ministry through merger, the reasoned arguments of outsiders and bean counters should be ignored.

Selling the parsonage and/or agreeing to have the pastor live off site. Many small congregations have enjoyed a long history of having the pastor live next door to the church. A century may have passed since the day a young congregation scraped together enough money to buy a piece of land and construct three buildings; a church, an outhouse, and a parsonage. In many places the economy of the day dictated that the parsonage be attached to the church so that the preacher needed to step outside only to use the outhouse. As times have changed the plumbing has moved inside, and the original parsonage may have been converted to Sunday school rooms or demolished for parking, and replaced by a house within a few blocks. What has remained fixed in many people's minds is the image of church and parsonage beside each other. They assume that it is convenient for the pastor, an idea that has been carried forward from horse and buggy days. I currently drive about twenty-five minutes to my church workplace, which is on par with the average commute of parishioners. I find that the drive time to church helps to provide a quiet space to organize my thoughts and that the return journey allows me to detach from the parish and deal better with my personal life. The hospitals and district meetings I attend are usually on the way or closer to my home. I have frequently encountered among small congregations an unhealthy desire to exert control over the pastor through their ownership of his or her housing. Some people enjoy keeping the pastor and parsonage family where they can watch them. Privacy has become such an important issue for my family that I am willing to accept reduced compensation, if only I can live where I choose. In today's era of cell phones and internet access, the availability of the pastor is not increased by having adjacent housing. The one exception to this is if the particular aspects of the church's ministry to the community require that pastor to be a resident. I know of a small inner city church that engaged in an active economic ministry to the impoverished of its neighborhood by operating a food bank and other services. When the violence of the neighborhood threatened the safety of the pastor's family, they allowed her to move out and purchase a suburban home. This pastor responded gratefully and took the initiative to maintain a high degree of visibility in the community. The success of the economic ministries was not affected in this case, but I can easily imagine a less intentional pastor failing to establish the trust needed by this situation.

For many small churches, the transition to not having the pastor next door is a threatening change to consider. I am suggesting that the leadership explore this option as a change that involves elevating one value, the health and effectiveness of their pastor, over other traditional and now less important values, such as depending on the pastor to turn out the lights left on at the church. The changing aspect of our society means that values sometimes come into conflict. Many small churches can realize great benefits from changing the housing component of its clergy compensation package.

The factors that drive small churches to relinquish their parsonages are likely to increase in the coming decade. Some churches need to demolish their housing in order to provide parking or room for building expansion. Many congregations will find their most suitable new pastor has a reason for not living in the parsonage. They may be part of a clergy couple or have a family member with a disability, allergy, or other special need which excludes the parsonage. As congregations explore shared ministry or become yoked to provide for clergy compensation, flexibility about clergy housing will be important to the negotiations. In the future more and more second-career and bi-vocational clergy will serve the smaller congregations. For them, giving up their current home in order to live in the parsonage will not be an option. A final factor is that if the congregation is engaged, as my current situation is, in an expensive expansion or reshaping of its ministries, then selling the parsonage may provide needed cash. Cash may open up a door for new ministry and keep the church in the game.

Entering a shared ministry. For reasons described at the end of chapter three, nearly every small church today will be transitioning away from the one-church-one pastor model. It would be very easy for those of us who love the small church to feel disillusioned and complain that rising clergy compensation costs are ruining the church. Shared ministry is such an exciting new avenue being opened to today's congregations that I think we should stop complaining and get with the program God seems to have for us. When negotiations about shared ministry face deadlines because of the need to provide a particular clergy compensation package, they rarely go well. The better process is driven by vision. It begins with discovering our shared values and how a mutual ministry might help us to achieve God's purpose for the church. The relationships are built first; the structure and the financial arrangements are considered much later. This process needs time. It also is better facilitated by a trained church consultant who is familiar with the literature, such as *Partnersteps* (Discipleship Resources).

Developing a new mission direction or program, such as, a food bank, latch key ministry, prison outreach, etc. There is currently a large amount of money available through government and private grants for the establishment of new faith-based initiatives. Churches should not enter into these projects with the idea that these grants will provide a way they balance their budget. What the church promises to give in exchange for a grant to start a new program is a tremendous investment in terms of volunteers. Taking on a grant-supported project is like deciding to have an elephant as a house pet. The presence of any new program will alter the church's sense of self-identity. The motivation to move in this direction must stem from the congregation's appreciation of a need that is being unmet in the community. If the desire to show compassion drives the ministry, then the money needed will be found. This being said, the smaller congregation often is the one in the community that has the courage and the skills to transform itself on behalf of those who are in need.

The Steps of Transition

Think about the transformation of a caterpillar to a butterfly. The caterpillar before the change knows only the steady life of munching across the marigold. Its size and position in the garden changes so slowly that it doesn't notice change at all. It doesn't have to consider new ideas or think about God's timing for life or the meaning of rebirth. God does have other plans for the caterpillar, but they are far from its awareness. It simply chews along week by week. God doesn't disturb the caterpillar's meal by showing it the transformed state. If the caterpillar had a vote at this stage, it would consider any change of that scale to be unnatural.

For me the exciting thing about caterpillars becoming butterflies is the mysterious way in which the minds become rewired. Think about it: when a caterpillar becomes a butterfly, every neuron must be switched. Not one part of the caterpillar is the same part in the butterfly. A whole new set of behaviors must be acquired on the fly. The caterpillar's world is two dimensional: just caterpillar and the flat plane of the leaf. The butterfly's world has three dimensions plus the wind. The mental change is far more incredible than the physical transformation.

For small churches the changes listed in the previous section are great transformations. They don't just happen by the council taking a vote and then that's it. Instead the people have to change mentally. They have to wrap their spirits around a different way of doing church. Also consider some of the transformations talked about earlier in this book. What about climbing the ladder to a higher level of community (chapter 5), rekindling spiritual passion (chapter 4), or dealing with a serious case of clergy misconduct (chapter 4)?

In the caterpillar the transformation is surrounded by a process. In small churches loving relationships are kept intact when proper process is followed. But if the pastor or someone else tries to skip the process and jump right to the physical reality of the change, the people will feel dis-empowered and alienated from their congregation. My earlier book, *The Church Transition Workbook* (Discipleship Resources, 2004), presents both the process and the resources needed to manage change. The following steps should be helpful to small churches as they go through transition:

1) Begin with an honest understanding of your current status. If the change has already been decided, declare a period of transition in which the congregation will work together to adapt to the change. Focus now on the church's purpose and sense of self-identity.

2) Research your history and attempt to see the present challenges in light of the past. If something will be lost in the transition, find ways to honor the contribution of that thing to the congregation's life. If, for example, the change involves relocating into a different building, provide time for people to remember and recognize the significant things that were a part of life in the old building. Get people involved in identifying which objects they can take with them into the new place. Provide time for grief.

3) Do a careful survey of what may hold the church back from growing. What are the weak areas of its program? Which of the causes of airplane crashes discussed in chapter four were of the greatest concern to your church's leadership? Enter into serious prayer for discernment as to the churches direction and needs.

4) Carefully communicate the implications of the change. Wait until the most respected members of the congregation come on board with the change, then let those people convince the majority to join them in supporting the change. Are there examples nearby of other small churches who have made a similar change? Send out scouting parties and let them report what they saw to the congregation. Allow time for people's concerns to be addressed.

5) Take action. As you prepare to step out and make the change, support it in worship. Focus on how the faithful people of the Bible took risks. Celebrate the first signs of success. Continue with an emphasis on praise and thanksgiving.

Small membership churches tend to have difficulty with changes that challenge their current "plan for survival." For the transition process to be completed, the congregation's mind has to shift to a new plan for survival. Their old plan might have involved having a certain amount of money in the bank. Their new plan might involve having a building which has been remodeled to meet their needs and sharing that building with the community. People will need their questions answered before they will accept that the new plan will work. I don't know how caterpillars come to trust the new form of security that flight offers them. I do know, however, when people spend time in prayer, their minds are often transformed to the place where they can make a similar leap of faith and support major changes to the church.

The Hopeful Future

As I have reflected upon the current state of the small membership church and then try to predict where they may be ten, twenty, of fifty years down the road, I find myself coming back to three questions which began this chapter. Each of these questions have implications for the local church, as well as implications for the denomination.

First, are the small churches, which today dot the American landscape, locked into the downhill side of a cycle of age and decline which will, in the end, lead to their being closed? The graying of the mainline church congregation is a concern which extends to large churches, as well as small ones, but the small congregation exists closer to the margin. A few funerals will put many small congregations out of existence. The statistics are bleak. The only thing that makes me optimistic is the unexplainable capacity of small congregations to be reborn. In hundreds of locations all over the country, small congregations are finding within themselves the courage to undergo great transformations. But, I believe that, for many, this transformation will be on hold until they successfully negotiate their entrance into a shared ministry. Once a congregation embraces a partnership with other churches, their sense of purpose, spiritual passion, and energy return. They will cease to be clergy dependent and will become lay empowered. These new covenant relationships will hold tomorrow's small churches much more accountable for ministry in their context. They won't be allowed to forsake their neighborhoods the way many churches of all sizes do today.

Those in denominational leadership need to be much more critical when they listen to the church growth experts who dismiss the role that small and long established congregations will play in the future. To be supportive of these churches, the denominational leaders must move away from their traditional one church-one pastor way of viewing ministry. To avoid the Life Cycle, denominations will also need to be reborn.

Second, where will small churches find the kind of leadership which is *open to change?*The answer to this question is really under our own noses. As long as clergy are sent to churches to do ministry to the people, the laity will find themselves in an adversarial role. But if clergy can shift their role to that of being team leaders who empower laity, all the leadership needed for change will bubble up. The Holy Spirit has already gifted God's people to serve him in new ways. Lay people will find great enjoyment in leading their own congregations through transitions, if these changes give them an opportunity to use what God has placed in their hearts.

Denominations must shift away from the representative democracy model that envisions clergy as extensions of the denomination's authority in the local church. The way in which we define ordination must shift away from set clergy-versus-lay roles and tasks. We need instead to train and place clergy people as team leaders, charged with building community and guiding the laity to discover their own gifted-ness to do ministry. Instead of working to elevate and segregate the professional clergy in opposition to the laity, denominations need to accept the ambiguity and equality which scripture gives those roles. Denominations also need to support the small membership church as they explore shared ministries across denominational lines.

Third, what about those small churches who today are at decisive points in their existence? Will they become sea squirts or butterflies? The good news is that every small congregation will soon face a decisive moment of transition. The bad news is that many small congregations will not choose wisely. There is little to be done to stem the tide of thousands of congregations who will close or merge in the decade ahead. The decision to change in ways that will lead to new life and vitality is not one that can be made for them. There are congregations which cannot be saved, not because they lack the resources, but because they lack the will. I am optimistic because I feel that the witness of those small congregations who are able to be transformed will have profound influence on the next generation.

Denominations need to invest in those tools and people who can help congregations through periods of transition. For churches who have experienced the kinds of "pilot error" mentioned in chapter 4, there needs to be a cadre of trained interim ministers ready to go into the situation. The process of negotiating a shared ministry also often requires a church consultant to be paid to work with the congregations. Much of this is up-front investment, where the denomination will need to foot the bill until the new form of ministry is established.

1 The most easily available is *The Life Cycle of a Congregation* by Martin F. Saarinen, which can be purchased online as a download from the Alban Institute (alban.org, copyright 1986, 2001). See also *Shaping a Future for the Church in the Changing Community* by Jere Allen and George Bullard (Atlanta, Home Mission Board, Southern Baptist Church, 1981) and *To Dream Again* by Robert D. Dale (Nashville, Broadman Press, 1981),

2 *On Death and Dying* by Elisabeth Kubler-Ross, MD. (Scribner; Reprint 1997).

Postscript

Holy Places

One of the most powerful models for the small church is that of a village of prayer. Prayer is one of those activities that seems to work better in small groups. Size may be an obstacle. When large churches seek to have an effective prayer ministry, they organize the ministry by assigning prayer tasks to small groups.

Jesus taught prayer primarily as a private discipline. He said, "But when you pray, go into your room, close the door and pray to your Father, who is unseen (Matthew 6:6 NIV)." Having established the intimate nature of prayer, he went on to teach what we know as the Lord's prayer using plural pronouns (our, us... "forgive us our sins as we..."). His only large-crowd prayers are either short prayers of thanksgiving or statements of faith. Jesus' longest prayer, recorded in John 17, is in the context of the small intimate group of his disciples. When Jesus faced his greatest prayer challenge, the night of his betrayal, he first pulled his faithful friends away from the crowd and into a place of seclusion, then he took three from the twelve to go a little further, and then he went off by himself and prayed a long time. The principle seems that when the crowd is large, the prayer is short (and more of a statement than a prayer); when the group is small, the prayer life is large and the spirituality intense.

I began this book by stating that our country is in the middle of a cultural shift that may bode well for the small membership church. People are today once again seeking to join intimate fellowships, like small congregations, where everyone knows your name. While it may be too early to find much statistical support for this, and the consumer driven mindset of today's young adults continues to favor the program offerings of larger churches, the high level of member satisfaction and commitment indicates a renewed vitality sweeping through many small churches. But I see an even deeper philosophical shift that needs to be noted. For the last century religious thought has been embroiled in a life or death struggle against the materialist assertions of modernity. The insights of Darwin, Nietzsche, Freud, and Marx have challenged not just the way Christianity is perceived by academics, but the usage made of faith in day-to-day life. The last two-thirds of the twentieth century have not been kind to the small church. With the very roots of the belief system under siege, Christians have fled like mediaeval villagers into the fortifications of a walled city or to the safety of the large churches. In the recent decades non-denominational megachurches have sprung up, sometimes using simplistic end runs around the deep philosophical issues of modern thought. In doing so, they appear to be effectively going on the offensive. The ground that large churches are currently gaining, however, may not be related to how well they answer the secular humanism, but rather, as we have mentioned before, the attractiveness of their programs to a consumer-driven society. The pendulum is swinging back in the favor of the small church's voice.

Twentieth century thought is being defeated, not by academic argument, but by the deep felt longing of our collective soul. Wherever you look in today's culture, you see a renewed interest in the spiritual. This may be the kind of spirituality that popularizes speculation about guardian angels, reincarnation, and the healing power of crystals. But there is also a return to seeking God as the one who can reveal our purpose for being and the meaning of life. Study Bibles and books, such as *The Purpose Driven Life*, are once again selling briskly. What this means for the small church is a renewed interest in prayer and other spiritual disciplines. People want to be guided so that they too can experience faith in day-to-day life. The small church with its principle of simplicity and its focus on how the gospel can be lived out in the midst of a community, which is willing to keep one accountable for one's faith, will connect with many of today's spiritual seekers. The small church is the right size for people who seek a place which practices intercessory prayer and offers to personalize the study of the scriptures so that they apply to day-to-day life.

These newcomers will be less interested in universal philosophical truth and more inclined towards discussions in which participants (particularly the laity) share their own personal experience of the Holy. Small churches will welcome these searching souls. They will be like scattered villages of prayer, little oases in the midst of a wilderness of secular values. Some of the small church values that we mentioned in the first chapter are likely to grow more popular in the next century. The fact that most small churches have remained faithful to such fundamental habits as worship, prayer, and fellowship, will serve them well. The small church's emphasis on the local over the universal will complement the culture's emphasis on experience over reason.

The small church, however, will continue to disappoint those who wish the congregation to be more task oriented and "purpose driven." They also, will disappoint those who come expecting the church to drop the exclusive claims of the Christian faith. Jesus' words, "I am the way and the truth and the life. No one comes to the Father except through me, (John 14:6 NIV)" may become the litmus test of small church membership. Those who are accepting of this claim will find their faith nurtured by the intimacy of a congregation whose life is spent exploring that way. Those who wish for a more universally inclusive theology are likely to travel on, bypassing the small congregation.

This is not a significant problem. Small congregation have long understood the implications of Jesus' prayer that we act as people who have been sent into the world, but who are not of the world (John 17:14-18). This is a distinction which seems easier to maintain when you have found the middle way of an intimate fellowship. It is interesting that whenever Jesus wanted to illustrate this principle of remaining true to one's purpose and changing the world, he chose something small. He taught about the salt of the earth (Matthew 5:13). The small church is indeed like grains of salt which alter the character of the community around them without losing their own saltiness. Jesus spoke about the leaven which raises the dough and the mustard seed, which was the smallest of all seeds (Matthew 13:33, 31). He also pointed to the widow and her mite, and he said that it was the greatest of all gifts (Mark 12:42). Each of these sayings can also be read as compliments which Jesus might say to the small congregation today. Each one, in a sense, tells the struggling church to hold on, and the faithful people to remember their purpose for being in a fellowship together.

The Six Truths

Why am I optimistic about the future of the small church?

1. The small church is an important part of a total strategy for reaching out with the saving gospel of Jesus Christ. The successful denomination of the future will provide appropriate clergy and in other ways support a diversity of church sizes. The small church has an important missional niche in our culture, and even the microsized congregation of a few dozen souls holds a vital part of the line against the advance of irreligious secularism.

2. Small churches have the intuitive wisdom to maintain their balance in the midst of changing economic times and the adverse social climates. To do this churches need to scale their programs, facilities, and clergy expectations to fit the number of people who presently attend their services. The day is gone when small congregations can afford to heat vast structures to preserve a remembrance of past glory. To help the small church, denominations must stop the unhealthy practice of sending a seminary-trained clergy as sole pastor for a small congregation. Shared ministries and bi-vocational clergy provide a much more sustainable service to these congregations.

3. Simplicity is the watch word for the healthy small church. Because small churches have established an intimate simplicity of relationship with those within their walls, they have the freedom to be more com-

plex in their relationships with other congregations and with mission projects.This flexibility makes their shared ministries an exciting part of the future religious landscape.

4. Each of the factors that cause small congregations to lose vitality and to fail can be addressed. There is nothing wrong with the average small congregation that cannot be fixed. An emphasis on health, rather than growth, will help small churches direct their efforts towards improving that which really needs to be improved.

5. Lay leadership, community, and teamwork can be built more easily in the small membership church than in larger churches. The smaller congregations will first grasp that a team approach to laity-clergy relationships makes more sense than the representative democracy model.

6. The small church has a hopeful future because, by God's grace, every congregation can be transformed. Small churches are not doomed to decline and die. They will not become like sea squirts stuck to their rocks. Many churches, if not most, will transition so that they can continue to minister to their communities.

The small church is a holy place. It is a space for prayer, for the preaching of the gospel, for the transforming action of the Holy Spirit. In some ways, being small helps these congregations stay closer to the spiritual needs of their people. The small church is not like the mid-sized church which positions itself near to some denominational standard in order to accept a normal, one clergy–one church placement. The small church is free to alter its clergy needs to fit its context. Because they go unnoticed by the denominational headquarters, they are often free to choose their own dance partners for shared ministry. They might even look for partners across denominational lines or enter into a relationship with a mission agency.

The small congregation also is not like the large church which has to keep running, with meetings and programs. The small church does not have to offer something for everyone.

The small-membership church needs to continue as a holy place, a village of prayer, gathered in this space and in this time to minister in response to the loving call of Jesus Christ.

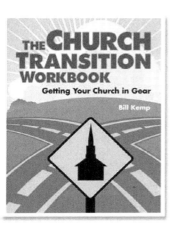

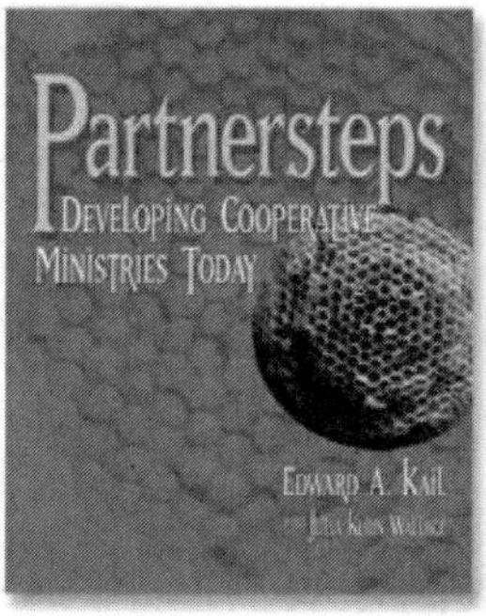

Partnersteps

Developing Cooperative Ministries Today

By Edward A. Kail with Julia Kuhn Wallace

The ministry of making, sustaining, and deploying Christian disciples is enhanced by missional partnerships and cooperative styles of ministry. *Partnersteps* provides theoretical concepts and practical information for the development of shared ministries. It offers examples of creative ministry partnerships plus exercises and group activities to apply the processes to your situation.

Edward A. Kail is the lead pastor of Faith United Methodist Church, a blended-ministry parish serving four communities in Humboldt County, Iowa. He was the first occupant of the Chair for Town and Country Ministries at Saint Paul School of Theology in Kansas City and taught church administration.

Julia Kuhn Wallace is a Christian educator who serves as Director of Small-Membership Church and Shared Ministries for the General Board of Discipleship of the United Methodist Church. In this consultative role she works with churches around the world.

ISBN: 0-88177-357-3

Equipped for Every Good Work

Building a Gifts-Based Church

By Dan R. Dick and Barbara Miller Dick

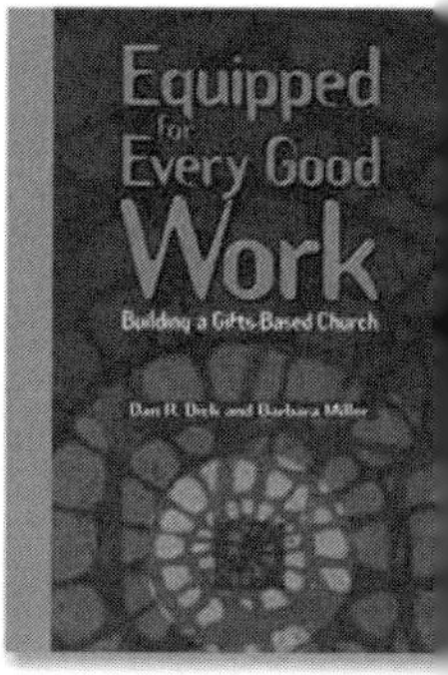

How can our church become more open and able to meet the ministry needs of the community? How do we maximize our potential without driving everyone crazy?

The four tools offered in *Equipped for Every Good Work* provide a way to explore this question and many others. The tools—Spiritual Gifts Inventory, Leadership/Interaction Styles, Spirituality Web, and Task Type Preferences—help individuals and groups discover and understand the gifts, attitudes, beliefs, and behaviors that influence their ability to live as Christian disciples and to lead within a community of faith.

Dan R. Dick is Director of Research for the General Board of Discipleship of the United Methodist Church. Barbara Miller Dick provides consultation, training, and resource development in spiritual gifts discovery, leadership development, change management, and conflict resolution.

ISBN: 0-88177-352-2